CONCILIUM

concilium

1991/5

RERUM NOVARUM
A HUNDRED YEARS
OF CATHOLIC
SOCIAL TEACHING

Edited by
John Coleman and
Gregory Baum

SCM Press · London
Trinity Press International · Philadelphia

October 1991

ISBN: 0 334 03010 2
ISSN 0010–5236

Typeset at The Spartan Press Ltd, Lymington, Hants
Printed by Dotesios Ltd, Trowbridge, Wilts

Concilium: Published February, April, June, August, October, December.

For the best and promptest service, new subscribers should apply as follows:
  US and Canadian subscribers:
Trinity Press International, 3725 Chestnut Street, Philadelphia PA 19104
Fax: 215–387–8805
  UK and other subscribers:
SCM Press, 26–30 Tottenham Road, London N1 4BZ
Fax: 071–249–3776

Existing subscribers should direct any queries about their subscriptions as above.

Subscription rates are as follows:
United States and Canada: US$59.95
United Kingdom, Europe, the rest of the world (surface): £34.95
Airmail to countries outside Europe: £44.95

Further copies of this issue and copies of most back issues of *Concilium* are available at US$12.95 (US and Canada)/£6.95 rest of the world.

Contents

Editorial: A Tradition to Celebrate, Criticize and Bring Forward

It would have been impossible to let the hundredth anniversary of *Rerum Novarum* pass by without a special *Concilium* commemorative issue. We want to celebrate *Rerum Novarum* as the starting point of an important, indeed precious, tradition of Catholic social thought on the economy, politics and world order and peace which has served as a serious alternative and corrective to secular liberal and socialist understandings. At the forefront of that tradition stands the radical primacy of human dignity and human solidarity as correctives to mere technocratic understandings of the economy and politics.

To be sure, Popes before Leo XIII addressed the social question. Gregory XVI's *Mirari Vos* and *Quanta Cura* and Pius IX's *The Syllabus of Errors* spoke to changes wrought by the French Revolution and the new bourgeois liberties and doctrines of the separation of church and state. The modern papal encyclical tradition really dates from 1740 with Pope Benedict XIV. In hindsight, we tend to find it fashionable to see these earlier papal judgments as one-sidedly reactionary. Yet, we might do well to reconsider and re-evaluate the wisdom in these earlier, pre-Leonine, papal 'no's to modern liberalism.

These Popes spoke a loud 'no' to an excessive individualism which broke up a larger solidarity; a decided 'no' to schemes to privatize religion and keep it entirely within the sacristy; 'no' to an espousal of a liberty of rights which allowed no clear corresponding duties; a resounding 'no' to positivism in law and political science and economics which would divorce the economy and polity (as impersonal and technocratic mechanisms) from moral scrutiny and human measure; a strong 'no' to a theory of civil rights which thought that economic rights, in Jeremy Bentham's terms, was 'nonsense on stilts'.

Recently, Michael Schuck, who also contributes an essay in this volume, has persuasively shown a coherence in this Roman Catholic papal social teaching reaching back from 1740 to the present.[1] Popes before Leo XIII adjured monarchical encroachments on the freedom of the church and rejected civil violence against secular states. They addressed family life and practices which threatened marriage and adolescent education. They condemned immoral business practices (e.g. excessive usury) and theft. *Mirari Vos* responded to Jeremy Bentham's utilitarian calculus for the social good of the greatest number. Gregory XVI retorted, 'every law condemns deliberately doing evil simply because there is some hope that good may result'. Pre-Leonine Popes set themselves against the social contract theory and unbridled capitalist market economies. Schuck argues that we lose something when we arbitrarily assign *Rerum Novarum* as the first of the social encyclicals. He comments, 'By limiting analysis to a conventionally designated set of "social" encyclicals, previous commentators have missed other letters of social relevance which aid interpretation of papal social thought as a whole.'[2]

Schuck notes:

> On one level, the discussions are dissimilar: pre-Leonine period encyclicals portray the world as a nourishing, yet dangerous pasture; Leonine period letters picture the world as a benign, cosmic hierarchy of being; post-Leonine period texts view the world as a temporal context wherein God and humanity journey together. Yet despite these shifting viewpoints, the popes collectively construe the world as a medium of God's ubiquity. Whether pictured as a pasture, a cosmos, or unmarked path, the world is imbued with God's presence. Monica Hellwig discusses this characteristically Roman Catholic perspective when she says: 'There is no realm whatsoever outside the dominion of that God.' She continues, 'Neither politics nor economics, neither national interests nor international affairs, neither technology nor commerce, neither aesthetics nor productivity, can ultimately be a law unto itself.' As a result, the popes uniformly criticize world views inspired by atheistic naturalism and dialectical materialism.[3]

The unity and coherence of this corpus of papal encyclicals, dating from 1740, argues Schuck, lies neither in Thomistic natural law theory (absent in the pre-Leonine corpus) nor in images of human dignity (not strong before the 1940s), but in a view of the world as pregnant with the presence of God; in an understanding of the objectivity of moral values and deep concern for protecting the family, religion and God's purposes for creation; in a sense of unity between the secular and the sacred, their nexus in God's ubiquitous presence.

Still, by common consent, *Rerum Novarum* inaugurated a special new beginning for Catholic social thought, and thus represents a kind of *magna carta* for modern social Catholicism. Popes subsequent to Leo – frequently on the very anniversary of the promulgation of *Rerum Novarum* – have updated, revised or revisited its analysis in the light of changing economic and political conditions.

Unlike other areas of theology, Catholic social teaching represents a distinctively evolving tradition, open to history and new data. To be sure, Catholic social teaching uses norms of judgment and standards for the orientation of action derived from the gospel and human experience. But the teaching itself has evolved through history and learned from some of its mistakes (e.g. the romance with corporatism in the earlier part of this century; shifts in the understanding of private property as proposed by Leo XIII; a reversal by John XXIII of earlier papal opposition to worker co-determination schemes). Catholic social teaching has been frequently inductive in its methodology and remains concerned about reading the signs of the times. It is an arena, pre-eminently, of the development of doctrine.

Just as the Popes themselves have re-evaluated the tradition over the years, the authors in this issue were challenged to do the same. They were asked not merely to celebrate the tradition as it already exists but to evaluate it for any *lacunae* or blind spots and to point to areas of change already achieved and those which may still need to be incorporated into the tradition.

In the first section of this issue we present essays which show how the Catholic social teaching responded to real social movements of socially concerned Catholics. M. Schäfers documents the debates and movements in the German-speaking world which led up to the document and asks what the church's teaching would have been like if, with Bishop Willem von Ketteler of Mainz, it had agreed that the time was ripe for moral pronouncement in 1870 instead of waiting until 1891. In Germany and Holland, the church opted for confessional labour unions. But in the Anglo-Saxon world, where both England's Cardinal Manning and Cardinal Gibbons of Baltimore in the United States had urged the Holy See to support the rights of labour, the unity of the workers' movement was not divided by confessional unions.

J. M. Díez-Alegría and Norbert Mette take up two very central themes of Catholic social teaching, already present in *Rerum Novarum*: property and the relation of Catholicism to socialism and capitalism. They show the development and shifts in understanding of these two central motifs through a one-hundred-year history. John Gallagher traces the two sources of Catholic social teaching – natural law and the gospel – and differing interpretations of their inter-relation. Michael Schuck treats of ideological uses of Catholic social teaching and the way it can be conceived of as a kind of ideology. Gregory Baum argues for the originality of this tradition in modern social thought in its three concepts of a democracy which applies to all societal institutions, the option for the poor and the notion of work as a *cultural* good.

In the second section we cover the reception of Catholic social teaching in different lands and among different groups. Essays deal with competing interpretations of this tradition in Germany, Italy, Poland and the United States, and its reception by feminists in the church and by liberation theology.

By this kind of reception hermeneutics it is possible to study how papal social teaching was received in different countries, and within these countries by different interest groups. In some parts of the world *Quadragesimo Anno* (1931) was used only as an authoritative anti-socialist statement or as the endorsement of corporatist schemes of economy. In the United States, however, it was used by the Catholic Church in support of Roosevelt's controversial reformist legislation, the so-called New Deal.

In countries that have Christian Democratic or equivalent Catholic parties, papal social teaching tends to be used as ideological support for these parties and their social philosophy. Catholics to the left of these parties then offer a critical reading of papal teaching, one that emphasizes its inherent ambiguities and sets forth the internal reasons why this teaching lends itself to ideological exploitation.

The reading of papal social teaching offered by Latin American liberation theologians has varied, depending on historical circumstances. When the option for the poor was supported by a confident, expanding liberation movement, ecclesiastical social teaching at first was seen as a handicap, but when the option for the poor came to be upheld by an embattled remnant, the same ecclesiastical documents were seen as supplying some support and protection.

In North America, progressive Catholics have offered a more positive reading of the papal encyclicals, and this for several reasons. There are no Christian political parties in North America. Since in the past Catholics were a powerless minority, at one time even despised, the established powers were not likely to use Catholic teaching to bolster their political cause. Another deeper reason for the more positive reading of papal teaching by American Catholics is the omnipresence of Lockean political thought, liberal individualism and utilitarian ethics in the United States and the scanty supply of collectivist intellectual traditions that transcend possessive individualism and support social solidarity. In this context, the Catholic tradition of social solidarity and the common good is invaluable, evoked even by non-Catholics as a potent resource to counteract the dominant language of atomistic social existence.

Over the past two decades the American and Canadian bishops have used this teaching in pastoral letters that severely criticized the ideology, culture and present orientation of the national economy.[4] In North America, then, the bishops and those progressive Catholics who articulate the Catholic social teaching see it and use it as a counter-cultural tool. The spirit of the celebration of the hundredth anniversary of *Rerum Novarum* – at least for the developed world – might be caught in the words of the American bishops in their 1991 pastoral message, 'A Century of Social Teaching: A Common Heritage, a Continuing Challenge':

> Across this country and around the world, the church's social ministry is a story of growing vitality and strength, of remarkable compassion, courage and creativity. It is the everyday reality of providing homeless and hungry people decent shelter and needed help, of giving pregnant women and their unborn children lifegiving alternatives, of offering refugees welcome and much more. It is believers advocating in the public arena for human life wherever it is threatened, for the rights of workers and for economic justice, for peace and freedom around the world and for 'liberty and justice' for all here at home. It is empowering and helping poor and vulnerable people realize their dignity in inner cities, rural communities and in lands far away. It is the everyday commitment and tradition of countless people, parishes and programs and of local networks and national structures – a tradition of caring service, effective advocacy and creative action. At the heart of this commitment is a set of principles, a body of thought and a call to action called Catholic social teaching . . .
>
> It is the challenge of our Lord Jesus Christ who laid out our continuing challenge in the Sermon on the Mount. In 1991, let us explore together what it means to be 'poor in spirit' in a consumer society; to comfort those who suffer in our midst; to show mercy in an often unforgiving world; to hunger and thirst for justice in a nation still challenged by hunger and the homeless, poverty and prejudice; to be 'peacemakers' in an often violent and fearful world; and to be the 'salt of the earth and the light of the world' in our own time and place.

Heeding this bishops' call shows that there is no lack of future agenda and challenge as we start the second hundred years of Catholic social teaching!

John A. Coleman
Gregory Baum

Notes

1. Michael J. Schuck, *The Context and Coherence of Roman Catholic Encyclical Social Teaching*, Washington, DC 1991.
2. Schuck, 5.
3. Schuck, 308. The citation from Monica Hellwig comes from her *Understanding Catholicism*, New York 1981, 185.
4. Cf. Thomas Gannon (ed.), *The Catholic Challenge to the American Economy*, New York 1987; Gregory Baum and Donald Cameron, *Ethics and Economics: Canada's Catholic Bishops on the Ecocomic Crisis*, Toronto 1984.

Redemptoris Missio

We know that encyclicals are not best-sellers. *Redemptoris Missio*, too, would not be an exception, even though the sensational manner in which it was presented to the universal church has brought considerable attention to it. At the moment of writing, I envisage at least four possible responses from the usual few who read such documents, and two of them, I presume, will be negative.

First, we must expect some believers to 'receive' *Redemptoris Missio* as an official pronouncement on the *missio ad gentes* made by the See of Rome within the presently known boundaries of orthodoxy, assigning to every category of person and institution within the church its specific obligation to engage itself in the missionary mandate given by Jesus. Second, there are missionaries who are disheartened by the paradigm-shift that has taken place in mission theology and mission praxis in the so-called mission territories; they are bound to welcome *Redemptoris Missio*'s efforts to restore the old missiological paradigm.

Inquisitive students of church documents, however, would examine the genesis of the encyclical and notice certain discrepancies between the approach adopted by the Pontifical Council for Inter-religious Dialogue (PCID, which is alleged to have been invited to prepare the original draft) and the 'tunnel vision' of the Congregation for the Evangelization of Peoples (CEP), which called the tune when framing the final redaction, ignoring and even negating the expertise and the accumulated experience of the PCID. The tension between the two Vatican institutions will be monitored with apprehension by those who have witnessed the slow and steady advances made by the PCID in developing the Conciliar perspectives on mission and dialogue (cf. the *PCID Bulletin*, 1989, XXIV/3, No. 72, 362–76) and the contrary tendencies becoming alarmingly evident in the CEP. Granted that the primatial see has every right to be heard by all churches on matters of doctrine and practice, one wonders what authority this encyclical enjoys, even if it bears the papal seal. These would be the concerns of the third category.

A few theologians from South Asia and their collaborators – this is the category most affected – might treat the document with critical disdain. This is sad, but inevitable. The reason for this would not just be the text of the encyclical, but Cardinal Josef Tomko's official interpretation of it. Speaking at the Consistory on 5 April 1991 in his official capacity as the head of the CEP (cf. *Origins* 20, 1991, 753–4), he alluded to vaguely generalized opinions of some Asian theologians and made an unambiguous and unfortunate reference to India as the 'epicentre' of errors that the encyclical was meant to combat.

Thus, a document that would have passed unnoticed (as unfortunately happens when too many documents emanate in succession) has every chance of being greeted with a counter-offensive. This will only further diminish the already dwindling authority of the Roman See. The pastoral leadership that the local churches so eagerly expect from the vicariate of Peter is continually damaged by unsubstantiated accusations irresponsibly aired in high places.

Furthermore, the Cardinal's polemical introduction will turn the encyclical into a dangerous weapon – as *Humani Generis* was in its own day – in the hands of heresy-hunters who wait to curtail and even crush the creativity of Asian Christians who are facing, with pastoral courage and theological daring, a totally new reality. The Asian church has not forgotten the ill-advised ecclesiastical interventions in the case of De Nobili and Ricci. No amount of papal eulogies heaped on such men posthumously has brought back lost opportunities. History is a good teacher, but is the church a good learner?

No Indian theologian claims infallibility. But Indian theologians are heirs to an ancient cultural tradition which fostered open and unbridled controversy as a way of *allowing even error to take its own time to say the truth it is trying to say*. Such tolerance we are entitled to expect from the primatial church which was human enough to have a long record of mistakes in its pastoral and doctrinal history; it can surely be human enough to allow the local churches of Asia to struggle through the same path of trial and error!

The encyclical, therefore, provides a good opportunity – and I hope Asian theologians will seize it – to engage Roman Congregations no less than the theologians of other local churches in an honest conversation about the missiological and christological positions alluded to in the cardinal's address.

In this short space I cannot treat any of the questions that this particular encyclical raises for the third and the fourth category of believers. But *Concilium* hopes to bring out a special number in 1993, on the emergent theological perspectives of the Asian church. Perhaps an opportunity might be provided there to return to this topic in greater detail.

Aloysius Pieris SJ

I · Catholic Social Teaching: Sources and Themes

Rerum Novarum – The Result of Christian Social Movements 'From Below'

Michael Schäfers

Different assessments have been made of Leo XIII's first social encyclical, *Rerum Novarum*, right down to the present day. A great deal of attention was already being paid to it in the Catholic sphere immediately after its public appearance in 1891. Only a few days after the proclamation of the encyclical, translations were in circulation all over the world, and the editions may well have amounted to several million copies. Not only Catholic but also Protestant, socialist and liberal pamphlets and journals of different provenance, which were of decisive significance for the formation of public opinion at the end of the nineteenth century, printed extracts from *Rerum Novarum*; at their centre was above all a description and evaluation of the answers of the encyclical to the vigorously disputed 'social question'.

The German Catholic journals in the Rhineland and Westphalia described the measures commended by *Rerum Novarum* as 'a breakthrough' and the 'final solution to the social question', and welcomed the fact that social and political Catholicism was now supported by an official papal declaration 'in the battle against godless liberalism, socialism and Protestantism'. The comments of the liberal press on the appearance of the encyclical were clearly more restrained. The leading liberal journal *Neue Freie Presse*, published in Vienna, thought that, 'The respect which is inculcated by the figure of the present Pope, who towers well above the average, cannot prevent the open acknowledgment that his encyclical on the workers' question comes as a disappointment. The Pope's letter contains undisputed truths; it is full of the warmest love of neighbour; but in content it does not devote a single line to the reforms long achieved by practical legislation'[1] in Austria and Germany. The *Historisch-politische Blätter für das katholische Deutschland*, one of the most influential German Catholic journals on social policy in German, which was edited by E. Jörg and F. Binder, noted that while the social legislation called for by the encyclical to protect the workers had still in no way been achieved even in Austria and Germany (as the liberal press asserted), the necessary social and political initiatives called for the Pope had already been taken by the Centre Party. In this respect the papal encyclical really offered 'nothing new'.[2]

This verdict of the liberal and Catholic press seems fair in that above all in France, Belgium, Austria and especially Germany, where a social and political Catholicism had developed on the basis of the specific social and political situation, in the form of Christian social movements and the Centre Party respectively, the possible solutions indicated by *Rerum Novarum*, especially its approval of state intervention (RN 25ff.) and the uniting of workers in pursuit of their own interests (RN 36ff.), had already been developed in political action and Christian social movements. However, with their social and political involvement these movements played more the role of outsiders in the churches, and for a long time were regarded by the church hierarchy with mistrust which went even so far as open opposition.

So in this perspective *Rerum Novarum* is not only the result of a process of academic theological and philosophical discussion (as e.g. in the 'Geneva Association', the 'Conseil des études de l'oeuvre des cercles catholiques d'ouvriers', the 'Circolo dei studi sociali ed economichi', the 'Free Associa-tion of Catholic Social Politicians' and the 'Fribourg Union') or a process of redaction within the Vatican;[3] central elements in its content were de-veloped through the Christian social movements or in them.[4] Before Pope Leo XIII, the representatives of these social movements had already declared that the 'social question' was the special concern of the whole church, had been intensively preoccupied with it on their own account, and had worked out possible solutions which explicitly or implicitly found their way into *Rerum Novarum*. I shall amplify these assertions on the basis of the development of church and Catholicism in nineteenth-century Germany.[5]

The end of the church?

After the Reichsdeputationshauptschluss in Regensburg in 1803 the church in Germany became a 'poor church' as never before in its history. As a result of secularization[6] in Germany alone it lost 3 princely states, 20 dioceses, 280 monasteries and Christian foundations, 18 Catholic universities, land amounting to around 100,000 square kilometres with 3.8 million inhabitants, and income from property and leases amounting to around 22 million guilders. As well as suffering this material loss of power, at the same time the church almost completely forfeited its political power. This development was in no way interpreted as a liberation within the church but as 'plundering' the church and restricting its ancient rights. Although the Catholic church was in principle opposed to the modern states which were coming into being, this did not prevent it from setting up the new church order that was needed along the lines of the successful bureaucratic structure of these states with the typical characteristics of bureaucratization, hierarchies and centralization.[7] This process lasted all through the nineteenth century, and amounted to stripping the intermediary episcopal authorities of power in favour of a strengthening of the papacy.[8]

The 'laity' save the church

That the church did not finally lose its connections with 'semi-modernity'[9] was due above all to individual, usually intellectual 'laity', who after 1820 increasingly formed themselves into a 'church renewal movement' and founded journals which were important for the Catholic sphere. Those thinkers who maintained the link between Christian faith and political action and so had a positive influence on the 'climate' for the discussion of the 'social question', like Joseph Görres (1776–1848),[10] were particularly influential in the rise of the Christian social movements.

Adam H. Müller (1779–1829) and Franz von Baader (1765–1841) were the first Catholic social theorists to occupy themselves with the consequences of the capitalist economic system which were gradually becoming visible in the migration of the country population into the cities and the growth of pauperism. Here they were supported by experiences and reports from England. Müller, who was intensively occupied with the theory of Adam Smith (1723–1790), condemned the factory system as being directed against the organic structure of society. He argued that the liberal economic system degraded the worker to a commodity, the payment for which was wages. Baader recognized the political implications of the structure of society when he compared 'social culture' to a pyramid, at whose small 'apex there are only a few favoured ones, whereas the broad basis' of those with constitutional rights were excluded.[11] He consistently supported the 'right of the proletariat to relief in their life', but in accordance with his romantic and conservative ideas he believed that this could only be achieved in an organic and cooperative order of society. According to Baader, Christian love of neighbour was the real way of solving the workers' problem and the social question, so he called for the revival of the earliest Christian diaconate. Thus at a very early stage Baader stressed that a contribution to the solution of the social question could be made by the church only if the structure of the church's ministry were adapted to the social need and poverty of the 'proletariat'.

The demands made by Müller and Baader for a reorganization of state and business, which was to be along the lines of a modified model of the mediaeval classes and guilds, continued to have some influence on Christian social movements and Catholic social philosophy down to the end of the nineteenth century. It quite often distorted views of the real conditions in the industrial economy which was coming into being and which no longer began from the mediaeval economic principle of covering need but from that of maximizing gain. Granted, the estimation that the Catholic church was in a position to solve the social question only by a re-Christianizing of society no longer appears in *Rerum Novarum*, since state intervention was affirmed, but even large parts of *Rerum Novarum*, since state intervention was affirmed, but even large parts of *Rerum Novarum* remained rooted in a 'policy of re-Christianizing'. The church's possibilities of solving the social question and its means of doing so were clearly over-estimated even by Leo XIII (RN 22).

Professor Franz Joseph Buss of Freiburg (1803–1878) was far ahead of developments in Germany and the thought of the Catholic church. The youngest member of the Baden Landtag, in his speech of 25 April 1837 he drew attention to the social problems and was thus the first Catholic politician to call for state social legislation and an associated programme for economic structures. Buss noted that factories were producing 'a new kind of serfdom . . . The factory worker is the serf of a master who uses him up as a profitable tool and then throws him away when he is used up'; at the same time the factory worker is 'the serf of the machine'.[12] As a programme for economic structures Buss called for the strengthening of the independent craftsman through state support of the system of distribution and of agriculture. Among other things, state social legislation should initiate the establishment of vocational schools and finance aid in cases of illness and accident, extend the factory inspectorate and health inspections, restrict child labour, and prohibit work on Sundays and festivals.

Here Buss was making demands which, with a variety of modifications, played a decisive role for the whole of social and political Catholicism in Germany right down to the papal social encyclicals. Buss's insights into the structural interconnections of the new industrial economy which was coming into being were also important. In his speech he stressed: 'As the uncertain legal and political position of the workers is predominantly rooted in their unfavourable economic situation, in both legal and political terms help must be expected from the economic improvement of the workers."[13] So Buss recognized that both the real social need and the moral and religious indifference of the factory workers complained of by the church were not the cause but the consequence of the industrial revolution, and an improvement of the material basis of existence was a decisive step towards solving the workers' question. Only in the 1870s did Buss's early insight increasingly become established in the church and in Catholicism. For the moment, 'the trend in the German church was more towards regarding the social question as a "religious" one and responding to it by pastoral or at any rate only charitable measures'.[14]

Developments in charity and politics after 1848

The Catholic church tended to stand aside from the March 1848 revolution.[15] Except in the Baden region, where through appropriate agitation Buss had already mobilized some thousands of Catholics in a number of organizations and their mass petition of 1846 had compelled the dissolution of the second Baden chamber, the church had no basis on which to organize and, impressed by the military measures taken against the Catholic Swiss 'Sonderbund', lacked the political revolutionary awareness to be able to take an active part in shaping the political overthrow.[16] However, this did not prevent the German episcopate and Catholicism from appropriating the struggles towards freedom which were being waged by national, liberal, democratic and socialist groups, and taking a part in the process of political discussion. Social and political Catholicism profited especially from the freedom of the press, of association and of religion which had been achieved in the revolution; only now did it have the necessary conditions for mobilizing a mass base among church people. These rights first made it possible for the church 'at least in some spheres to follow the gradual pluralization of life in a modern society which was becoming increasingly complex, without excessively burdening structures of church ministry with modern aspirations of plurality'.[17] The institutional structure of the official church could continue to orientate itself on a modernized, hierarchical and absolutist model and claim the 'service of salvation' for itself, whereas the new democratic associations which needed to be founded were to take account of the new demands of the time through their 'service of the world'.

In 1848, the year of the revolution, a wider public in Germany became aware of the 'social question', but in the course of the political conservatism which followed they again lost sight of it. In the Catholic sphere it was above all W. E. von Ketteler (1811–1877), at that time pastor of the small Westphalian community in Hopsten and a Catholic delegate to the Frankfurt parliament, who stressed the special significance of the social question. In his speech to the first assembly of the Catholic Associations of Germany (the Katholikentag), Ketteler pointed out: 'The most difficult question, which has not yet been solved by any legal regulations and any forms of state, is the social question . . . It will prove that the final solution of the social question is reserved for the Catholic church; for no matter what regulations the state may make, it does not have the power.'[18] In the second of his famous advent sermons in the cathedral at Mainz, Ketteler stressed his attitude: 'So if we want to discern the time we must seek to fathom the social question. Anyone who understands it discerns the present, and to anyone who does not understand it, both present and future are a riddle.'[19]

According to Ketteler, the social situation of the time was characterized by the way in which there was 'hostile confrontation between the haves and the have-nots', 'the growth of mass poverty from day to day' and 'doubts in the popular mind about the right to private property'.[20] As early as 1848 Ketteler resolved the problem of property – as did *Rerum Novarum* later (RN 4f., 19f.) – with reference to revelation, Thomistic doctrine, the theology of original sin and natural law. Accordingly, Ketteler argued that in the Christian view human beings have 'only a God-given right to use the goods of the earth in the order that is prescribed by him, with the intent that all human beings should receive their necessary bodily needs from the fruit of the earth'.[21] In referring to the 'practical' grounds mentioned in Thomas, Ketteler argued for the individual's right to property, since an economic order in which property was held in common, of the kind striven for by communism, was not in accord with nature. Nevertheless, the right to property was not an absolute right, since 'God created nature to nourish all human beings, and this purpose must be achieved. Therefore each individual must again make the fruits of his property a common good, in order as far as in him lies to contribute to the achievement of this determination.'[22] Here Christian love of neighbour is enjoined for the poor.

Thus, like many of his contemporaries, Ketteler saw the solution to the 'social question' primarily in the establishment of charitable associations. This is understandable, given that in the first place industrial development was only just beginning in most of the Catholic areas[23] and was hardly of any help in a solution of the 'social question', and secondly that the church could refer to a long tradition of charity which had been well able to adopt itself to changing circumstances and social demands.[24] Nevertheless – as

O. von Nell-Breuning aptly noted –[25] this tradition of Christian charity had long prevented the breakthrough of a political Christian social movement concerned for structural reform by suggesting that a solution of the 'social question' could be achieved simply by church charity. In fact, because of social and political changes and of the changed self-understanding of individuals, church charity was no longer in a position to do this.

Moreover a solution to the social question was looked for in church circles from intensive priestly pastoral care and a 'reform of disposition', since – here we have a regression from the insights of Buss – 'pastoral and spiritual neglect' and the fall away from the church were regarded as the cause of the rise of the proletariat and pauperism. A contribution in 1854 to the journal *Der Katholik*, edited by J. B. Heenrich and C. Moufang, makes this clear. In principle, pastors were recommended to exclude from their parishes 'any kind of industry which necessitates great gatherings'.[26] If this was not possible, then the following pastoral measures were to be taken. The pastor was to call on 'the manufacturer to supervise the way of life of the workers in according with a specific rule, with the utmost strictness, and to promise him any permissible support; if this is not done, he should threaten the utmost opposition to the business'.[27] An obligation to go to mass on Sunday and a regulation of working hours were also important for pastoral care. Moreover there should be a mass every day at the beginning of work, after which the workers should be separated according to sex, and should go from the church to the factory praying the rosary, where they would all meet together punctually for work. If at all possible, only Catholics of the same sex were to work together in a room: 'the pastor must insist with all his might on the isolation of Catholics'.[28] Before and after work, and during breaks, prayers, scripture readings and stories of the saints should be recited. Funds for use in illness and savings banks should be established and administered after conversations between the factory owner and the pastor.[29]

It is obvious nowadays that these pastoral measures were hardly an appropriate way of coping with the ongoing struggle for political emancipation among industrial workers and of making at least a beginning of settling the social question. The reasons for the late rise and consolidation of a Catholic or Christian workers' movement relate not only to the rise of the Socialist workers' movement but also to the paternalistic spoon-feeding of industrial workers by large parts of the official church hierarchy, which kept them in subservience. The significance of this paternalistic attempt at a solution lies in the fact that it made a decisive contribution to the rise and stabilization of the Catholic 'pietistic movement' – largely organized by the Jesuits – which provided the mass basis for the claims of the Pope to political sovereignty ('the Roman question').[30]

The organized start

In the early period of industrial capitalism in Germany it proved possible to double industrial production and foreign trade between 1851 and 1860. The economic expansion continued after 1871, but this in no way led to an easing of the social situation; rather, the class struggle between wage-earners and capitalists markedly increased. Unemployment, housing problems, the use of female and child labour, wages below the minimum subsistence level and a lack of social security were only some of the factors which marked the situation of the workers in Germany. As a reaction to this development and the impoverishment of the proletariat in the cities there was an increase in the number of workers' organizations, which attempted to set up a 'counter-force', an 'emancipation and self-help movement', to combat the arbitrariness of the capitalists and state repression. 'Their concerns were a shortening of working hours, work-places commensurate with human dignity, protection from accidents at work, and mutual material help in the case of loss of jobs and changes of workplace. At a very early stage the idea also arose of improving the position of workers as consumers by co-operative organizations or even by putting production on an independent footing, free from exploitation. Social emancipation was expected from self-organized education.'[31] In 1863 F. Lassalle (1825–1884) founded the 'General German Workers' Association' in Leipzig, which in 1875 combined with the Social Democratic Workers Party founded in 1869 by A. Bebel (1840–1913) and W. Liebknecht (1826–1900) to form the 'Socialist Workers Party of Germany'.

On the Catholic side, Ketteler, who since 1850 had been Bishop of Mainz, continued to occupy himself intensively with the solution to the 'social question', and from September 1863 to spring 1864 worked on his *magnum opus*, *Die Arbeiterfrage und das Christentum*, which over the next few years was translated into a number of languages. In the book, which was conceived of as an answer to the publications of H. Schulze-Delitzsch (1808–1883) and F. Lassalle, [32] Ketteler stressed the need for a systematic social policy and social reform. At the same time he attempted to bring clarity to the economic market laws of prices and wages: 'This is the situation of our working class; it is dependent on wages; these wages are a commodity; its price is determined daily by supply and demand; the axis around which it moves is provided by the necessities of life: if demand is greater than supply, then it goes above this axis; if supply is greater than demand, it falls below it . . . '[33] Ketteler goes on to say: 'We can no longer deceive ourselves – the whole material existence of almost all the working class, and thus of by far the great majority of people in modern states, the existence of their families, the daily quest for the food needed for man, woman and child, is exposed to all the fluctuations of the market and the price of goods.'[34]

These comments contain clear parallels to Lassalle's theory of the 'iron law of wages'. Moreover both Ketteler and Lassalle saw the establishment of producers' associations as a contribution to the solution of the workers' question. In contrast to Lassalle, the Bishop of Mainz believed that the capital needed for these economically independent workers' enterprises could be obtained through giving, whereas Lassalle thought that state financing was necessary. Although Ketteler immediately made available 5000 guilders from his private resources for the associations to be set up, he could not collect enough money through gifts from middle-class Catholic circles. How close the relationship between the two individuals was is evident, among other things, from the fact that at Lassalle's request his long-time friend Sophie von Hatzfeld attempted to secure Bishop von Ketteler as a mediator between him and the family of Helene von Dönning. Lassalle promised that if Ketteler accepted the role of mediator, and the marriage between Lassalle and Helene von Dönning came off, he would go over to Catholicism in order to be able to marry Helene according to the Catholic rite. The death of Lassalle in a duel near Geneva in 1864 brought to an end not only the lines of communication between the Catholic 'workers' bishop' and the Social Democrat 'workers' leader', but also between social Catholicism and the socialist movement generally. Ketteler did not maintain his links with the socialist movement. One reason was doubtless the papal *Syllabus* of 8 December 1864, which caused Ketteler considerable difficulties over his credentials in the church ecause of his ties with Lassalle.

The 'forgotten tradition'

Between 1865 and 1870 the first 'Christian-social associations' spread, above all on the lower Rhine, in the Ruhr, in Aachen,[35] Elberfeld and Krefeld. 'These associations fitted well into the twin fronts held by the Catholics, against the Social Democrats, the "power of the workers without God", and against the liberals, "the power of money without religion" . . .'[36] However, this defensive position against socialism and liberalism in no way resulted in a defensive attitude to the political and economic events of the time; the 'Christian-social organizations' involved themselves in organizing strikes and attempts to organize the workers' interests in a way which transcended confessions and was independent of church supervision. Moreover, one of their leading ideas was the development of a 'religious socialism'. By 1872 the Christian social movements had 22,000 members and were thus numerically the strongest workers' organization in Germany. Their main demands included wage-rises, cuts in working hours, a prohibition of the employment of children and married women, funds to support those in social need, producers' associations and unrestricted freedom of association for workers. However, as early as the middle of the 1870s, unpolitical, Catholic and above all charitable associations became the model in the Catholic sphere. The final downfall of the 'Christian-social associations' was brought about by the police-state measures taken in the Kulturkampf and the 'socialists' law' of 1878, which affected not only the Socialist Workers Movement but all workers' associations. At the same time, even within the church hierarchy, no attempts were made to keep the Christian-social associations alive. Among other reasons, they were unpopular because of their political and in principle transconfessional commitment and their distance from the conservative wing of the Centre Party. R. Görner has rightly regretted that 'with the end of the Christian-social associations, one of the greatest opportunities of the church to win over the workers was lost'.[37] Furthermore, no attention was paid in *Rerum Novarum* to the discussion which began in individual groups of the Christian-social associations, and which took up the basic concerns of socialism.

Structural reform through a systematic social policy

By the latest at the end of 1865, Ketteler came to realize that the social question cou not be resolved by charitable measures alone, and from then on argued more clearly for the collaboration of the state and 'self-help' from the workers. In 1869 he had the opportunity to present his ideas about the solution of the workers' question to the German episcopate. Dismissing the kind of excuse constantly made in connection with the late appearance of *Rerum Novarum*, that the time for a discussion of the 'social question' had not been ripe before 1891, as early as 1869 Ketteler stressed to the German bishops' conference in Fulda: 'Here one could perhaps point out that the workers' question and its solution is still all too confused and not developed enough for the matter to be taken up by the church on a large scale, in due tranquillity and certainty, and with the hope of good success, at this stage. But such a view is completely wrong. The time is perfectly ripe.'[38]

Ketteler's demands were far-sighted: the need to include the treatment of the workers' question in the training of the clergy and to appoint church officials in the individual dioceses 'to compile statistics of the factories and factory workers in the diocese concerned, to gain information about their physical, intellectual, moral and religious situation and about the welfare of the workers and the associations and organizations created to improve their lot'.[39] These proposals, and Ketteler's whole speech, found little response in the German episcopate, which was preparing for the First Vatican Council and the debate on infallibility. Most bishops were unaware that the 'social question' related directly to the 'deposit of faith'.[40] At the same time there was still widespread mistrust among the official hierarchy of the 'militant self-help'[41] of the workers. Large parts of the Catholic church still believed that – as Leo XIII put it in *Quod apostolici muneris* (121) – 'having had enough of their poor dwellings or workplaces, the lowest classes are bent on attacking the palaces and goods of the rich'.

In 1870/71 the Catholic Centre Party formed itself into a faction in the Prussian Landtag and in the Reichstag. 'Although the Centre was founded as a political party, the programme put church and confessional perspectives firmly in the foreground. Interest in social problems was clearly articulated, but in principle the Centre was committed to preservation of the existing conditions in the field of tension between the three poles of capital, poverty and work, and openly opposed only obvious abuses in the situation of the workers.'[42] During the Kulturkampf, the social and political demands served the Centre above all as a means of fighting against Bismarck's anti-church policy. Nevertheless it was above all to the credit of the Centre Party that it had co-operated in the construction of a systematic social policy and the beginnings of viable social security before the appearance of the papal encyclical in 1891.

The beginnings of organization

At the end of 1889, a clear shift of accent can be noted in German social Catholicism. In reaction to the rapid rise of Social Democracy after the abolition of the 'socialists' law', the Catholics slowly arrived at an understanding with the liberal capitalist economy, which seemed to them more acceptable than the idea of socialist revolution. Forces stirred in the church which wanted to give up the defensive position towards society and state and the 'ghettoizing' of the church and Catholicism caused by the Kulturkampf, in favour of an active shaping of capitalism and removal of its structural deficiencies. Morever in church and Catholic circles there was an increasing awareness that the Catholic workers' associations, in which wage-earners and entrepreneurs could organize and support one another, harmoniously united by the bond of the Catholic faith,[43] were hardly enough to meet the needs for emancipation and organization among the workers with religious ties and to prevent the rise of the socialist trade union movement. To begin with, 'specialist divisions' were particularly favoured as new forms of organization. Building on the existing workers' associations, they were to bring together the workers by professional groups and to involve the clergy, with the aim of pursuing 'material professional interests'.[44] In addition to this, after 1894 the first Christian trade unions were founded, and in 1901 they finally came together in the 'General Alliance of Christian Trade Unions'. But this rise was hindered by the 'trade union dispute' within the church which followed.

Rerum Novarum

The social encyclical *Rerum Novarum* of 1891 confirmed the developments and the beginnings of the solution to the 'social question' which had taken shape within the German Catholicism of the nineteenth century and had been arrived at through disputes and class struggles in society and the church. Basic contents of the 'workers' encyclical', like the demand for state intervention and freedom of association for workers; the resolution of the property question with reference to Thomistic philosophy, natural law and revelation; and the anti-socialist and anti-liberal orientation, had already been developed in the Christian social movements before 1891. That the Christian social movements and the Catholicism of the church hierarchy were far ahead in decisive areas was because of their special position: they had come into being as a response to the pluralization of the modern world in the nineteenth century, took a direct part in the social and political struggles and movements of the time, and in so doing developed an ethic which could be adopted by the papal encyclical. The fact that not only the positive achievements of Christian social movements and Catholicism but sometimes also the defects in their political and social strategies and attempted solutions to the social question were handed down through *Rerum Novarum* shows the ambivalence of this process.

The great achievement of Leo XIII, who was concerned simultaneously with 'a Christianizing of modern life and a modernizing of Christian life' (J. Schmidlein), was to draw the attention of large areas of the public within the church to the workers' question, which hitherto had been treated only by individual representatives and groups within Catholicism and the Christian social movements. He thus supported the extension of the Christian workers' movement, especially by recognizing the workers' right of association. Moreover, *Rerum Novarum* obliged those church circles which were fixated on authority and hesitant or even hostile about workers organizing themselves to be concerned about the 'social question'. That the encyclical did not propose specific forms of workers' organizations and left open, for example, the questions of permissible working hours and the specific form of social insurance, thus passing over the discussions being carried on in the workers' movement, was an attempt to bind together different and sometimes divergent trends within the church and Catholicism by guidelines which were kept general and abstract. As the dispute over the interpretation of *Rerum Novarum* and the trade union dispute in Germany make clear, this did not prove successful.

From the perspective of the present day we can only speculate how the history of the nineteenth century and the church would have turned out had the papal encyclical on the social question appeared when Bishop Ketteler already thought the time ripe. The church recognized too late what the Jewish philosopher and revolutionary Rosa Luxemburg formulated in 1913 in her commemorative article on Karl Marx as the quintessence of Lassalle's activity: 'Human beings do not make their history out of freely available material, but they do make it themselves.'[45] One would want to add that they want to make it themselves and be responsible for it.

Translated by John Bowden

Notes

1. Quoted from F. Klüber, *Katholische Gesellschaftslehre* 1, Osnabrück 1968, 287.
2. *Historisch-politische Blätter für das katholische Deutschland* 108.1, 1891, 63–75: 73.
3. Cf. G. Antonazzi, *L'enciclica Rerum Novarum*, Rome 1957; H. Sorgenfrei, *Die geistesgeschichtlichen Hintergründe der Sozialenzyklika Rerum Novarum*, Heidelberg and Louvain 1976; I. Camacho, *La encíclica Rerum Novarum*, Granada 1984.
4. Cf. O. von Nell-Breuning, 'Christliche Sozialbewegung', *Stimmen der Zeit* 173, 1963/4, 1–9.
5. For the concept of 'Catholicism' in Germany cf. O. von Nell-Breuning, 'Sozialer und politischer Katholizismus', *Stimmen der Zeit* 193, 1975, 147–9; H. Katz, 'Katholizismus zwischen Kirchenstruktur und gesellschaftlichem Wandel', in *Zur Soziologie des Katholizismus*, ed. K. Gabriel and F. X. Kaufmann, Mainz 1980, 116.
6. Cf. K. Schatz, *Zwischen Säkularisation und Zweiten Vatikanum*, Frankfurt am Main 1986, 22ff.
7. Cf. M. N. Ebertz, 'Die Bürokratisierung der katholischen "Priesterkirche"', in *Priesterkirche*, ed. P. Hoffman, Düsseldorf 1987, 132–63.

8. Cf. F. X. Kaufmann, *Kirche begreifen*, Freiburg, Basle and Vienna 1979, 61; cf. H. Jedin (ed.) *The History of the Church*, Vol. 8, London and New York 1981.

9. Cf. K. Gabriel, 'Lebenswelten unter den Bedingungen entfalteter Modernität', *PthI* 8, 1988, 93–106.

10. Cf. B. Wacker, *Revolution und Offenbarung. Das Spätwerk (1824–1848) von Joseph Görres – eine politische Theologie*, Mainz 1990, 215f.

11. F. von Baader, 'Über das dermalige Missverhältnis der Vermögenslosen oder Proletairs zu den Vermögen besitzenden Klassen der Societät (Munich 1835), in *Texte zur katholischen Soziallehre* (= *TkS*), Kevelaer 1976, II. 1,47.

12. Speech by Franz Josef von Buss of 15 April 1837, on the social problem, *TkS* II.1, 65.

13. Ibid., 82.

14. R. Görner, 'Die deutschen Katholiken und die soziale Frage', in *Geschichte der Christlich-Demokratischen und Christlich-Sozialen Bewegungen in Deutschland*, ed. G. Rüther, Part I, Bonn 1984, 158.

15. Cf. W. Siemann, *Die deutsche Revolution von 1848/49*, Frankfurt 1985.

16. Cf. H. Hürten, *Kurze Geschichte des deutschen Katholizismus 19800–1960*, Mainz 1986, 79f.

17. R. M. Bucher, 'Katholische Verbände – Lernorte der Kirche', *Arbeiterfragen* 3/ 1990, 4.

18. W. E. von Ketteler, *Sämtliche Werke und Briefe*, ed. E. Iserloh, I.1, Mainz 1977, 18, 19.

19. Ibid., 35.

20. Ibid., 26.

21. Ibid., 28.

22. Ibid., 30.

23. Cf. M. Greschat, *Das Zeitalter der Industriellen Revolution*, Stuttgart, Berlin, Cologne and Mainz 1980; W. Schwer and F. Müller, *Der deutsche Katholizismus im Zeitalter des Kapitalismus*, Augsburg 1932, 7–76.

24. Cf. M. Mollat, *Die Armen im Mittelalter*, Munich 1984; B. Geremek, *Geschichte der Armut*, Munich and Zurich 1988.

25. Cf. Nell-Breuning, 'Sozialbewegung' (n.4), 2f.; id., 'Kirche und Arbeiterschaft', in *Unbequeme Grenzziehung. Streitschriften von Oswald von Nell-Breuning*, ed. I. Brusis and M. Grönefeld, Cologne 1990, 109.

26. 'Die Industrie und die Seelsorge in Fabriken', *Der Katholik* 34, 1854, 371.

27. Ibid., 372.

28. Ibid., 374.

29. Ibid., 375.

30. Cf. L. Grane, *Die Kirche im 19.Jahrhundert*, Göttingen 1987, 132f.; M. N. Ebertz and F. Schultheis (ed.), *Volksfrömmigkeit in Europa. Beiträge zur Soziologie populärer Religiösität aus 14 Ländern*, Munich 1986.

31. A. Klönne, *Die deutsche Arbeiterbewegung*, Cologne 1980, 40f.

32. Cf. H. Schulze-Delitzsch, *Capitel zu einem deutschen Arbeiterkatechismus*, Leipzig 1863; F. Lassalle, *Arbeiterlesebuch. Rede Lassalles zu Frankfurt am Main am 17. und 18.Mai 1863 nach dem stenographischyen Bericht*, in *Gesammelte Reden und Schriften*, ed. E. Bernstein, Vol.4, Berlin 1919, 111–69.

33. Ketteler, *Sämtliche Werke* (n.18), 379.

34. Ibid., 380.

35. Cf. F. Focke, *Sozialismus aus christlicher Verantwortung*, Wuppertal 1981, 35ff.

36. T. Nipperdey, *Religion im Umbruch. Deutschland 1870–1913*, Munich 1988, 56.

37. Görner, *Deutsche Katholiken* (n.14), 167.

38. Ketteler, *Sämtliche Werke*, I.2, Mainz 1978, 438.

39. Ibid., 450.

40. Ibid., 435.

41. Cf. A. Klönne, "'Kämpferische Selbsthilfe." Zur Tradition des Arbeiterkatholizismus', *Arbeiterfragen* 1, 1986.

42. K. E. Lönne, *Politischer Katholizismus im 19. und 20. Jahrhundert*, Frankfurt am Main 1986, 153.

43. Cf. J. Mooser, 'Arbeiter, Bürger und Priester in den konfessionellen Arbeitervereinen im deutschen Kaiserreich 1880–1914', in J. Kocka (ed.), *Arbeiter und Bürger im 19. Jahrhundert*, Munich 1986, 79–105.

44. Cf. M. Schneider, *Die christlichen Gewerkschaften 1894–1933*, Bonn 1982, 43f.

45. R. Luxemburg, *Gesammelte Werke*, Vol.3, Berlin 1980, 182f.

Ownership and Labour: The Development of Papal Teaching

Jose María Díez-Alegría

1. *Rerum Novarum*

Seen from our present viewpoint, the encyclical's teaching on ownership is very unsatisfactory. It roundly asserts, in opposition to the socialists, that possessing goods privately as personal property is a right given to human beings by nature. This right belongs to human beings since they are intelligent and rational, and therefore capable of foresight and providence with respect to the future. Hence they should be seen as having rights not only to consumer goods, but also to those which usage does not consume, and specifically, to land.[1]

Leo XIII, though without acknowledging it, seems here to be inspired by St Thomas Aquinas (2–2, q.66,a.1). But he is making a seriously erroneous interpretation. Thomas Aquinas does indeed devote the whole question 66 of his 2–2 to a thematic treatment of human dominion over things and the right to property. But he proceeds by parts. In a.1 he merely asks if it is natural for human beings to possess external things; he replies in the affirmative through the argument of the reasonableness of human nature. But he is not yet speaking of private property, since he poses this question in a.2, where he asks if human beings can legitimately possess anything as their own. According to Aquinas, the dominion that is 'natural' to human beings as rational beings is a basic dominion which could be realized in social forms; this would guarantee their personal participation in the use and reasonable disposition of goods.

Speaking now in a.2 of 'private property', and feeling the weight of a Christian tradition that is clearly reticent about this and leans rather to the holding of goods in common,[2] St Thomas replies with a distinction: with respect to the use of external things, men should hold these as though they were in common, placing them at the disposition of others. Concerning the power to provide or dispose of these goods, on the other hand, the régime of private property is licit and even necessary up to a point. This does not stem from reasons of metaphysical anthropology, however, nor even from ethical ones, but from pragmatic considerations of greater benefit and more peaceful co-existence.[3]

To return to *Rerum Novarum*: there is a certain contradiction between affirming that human beings as rational beings have a right to private property, including land, and accepting that the majority of humankind possess nothing more to live on than the wages earned by their labour.[4]

To prove that the right to private property is natural, *Rerum Novarum* argues that by working on a part of nature, human beings award this to themselves as private property, since their work leaves a sort of stamp on it.[5] Here Leo XIII's concept of private property coincides with John Locke's, but without an important reservation added by Locke: at least when there is enough of this commodity for others to have use of it. All this betrays a vision of human existence *à la* Robinson Crusoe, which does not correspond to the complexity of social and historical reality, or take account of the cultural and technical dimensions of labour and consumption in modern society.

Rerum Novarum's two most important contributions to the question of ownership and labour are its affirmation that justice requires that wages should be sufficient for the upkeep of a 'frugal and sober' worker,[6] and its proclamation of the right of workers to free association, including the autonomy of such associations.[7] Of wages, the encyclical notes that these are personal, but also necessary. Therefore, if a worker, forced by necessity, accepts inhuman conditions laid down by the employer or business, this is putting up with a violent injustice. Here Leo XIII is saying that the free market needs to be corrected by imperatives of justice. This is a viewpoint heavy with consequences.

2. *Quadragesimo Anno*

Forty years after *Rerum Novarum*, Pius XI repeated its teaching on private property in *Quadragesimo Anno*. Here, however, its 'social function' is stressed.[8] The solution proposed to make this effective is perhaps its teaching on the 'corporate order'.[9] But this proposal, made in a purely abstract way, turned out to be dangerously close to the syndicalist structure of totalitarian régimes (Italy, Portugal, Spain, Germany), which, while denying freedom of party and association, in fact submitted to capitalist interests. This is why later Popes, and the Second Vatican Council, without explicitly renouncing this aspect of *Quadragesimo Anno*, have left it aside. In any case, Pius XI had insisted on the right to free and autonomous associations.[10]

Concerning the just wage, Pius XI added a clarification to *Rerum Novarum*'s concept of a life-supporting wage: this should be sufficient reward to cover the human needs of the worker 'and his family'.[11]

3. Addresses by Pius XII

Pius XII, in his radio address of 1 June 1941, makes an interesting observation: 'Every man, as a living being endowed with reason, has in effect by nature the basic right to use the material goods of the earth, even when the detailed regulation of the practical application of this right is left to human will and the juridical authorities of nations.'[12] Here the social teaching of the church is once more connected to the great patristic and mediaeval tradition. Private property and the free reciprocal interchange of goods are subordinate to 'the natural end of material goods, and cannot be made independent of the primary and basic right, which concedes their use to all, but should rather serve to establish this right in conformity with this end'.[13]

Pius XII's teaching on private property is nevertheless laden with unresolved tensions, which emerge clearly from the radio address of 1 September 1944, the homily of 3 June 1950, and his 1952 and 1955 Christmas messages.[14] These texts clearly show an inadequate historical and social analysis and an excessive nostalgia for the world of peasants and guilds, seen as almost the only vehicles for safeguarding personal values. Such an outlook is of very little help in tackling the complex socio-economic problems of the modern world realistically.

With regard to labour, Pius XII reaffirmed the full right of workers to free trade unions[15] and the right to make one's labour the means of providing for one's own life and that of one's children.[16]

4. *Mater et Magistra* and *Pacem in Terris*

John XXIII's *Mater et Magistra* represents an advance on Pius XII's teaching on the subject of property. This advance consists in the historical and sociological analysis of modern industrial society and the roles played in it by social security systems, professional expertise and rights founded on labour.[17] The ability of businesses to finance themselves sometimes produces a social debt, and workers should be granted a share by way of credit, especially if they are being paid no more than a subsistence wage.[18] Steps should be taken to change businesses into true human communities, giving workers an increasing share of co-responsibility in their administration and development.[19]

Besides these analyses of the complex make-up of society, *Mater et Magistra* continues to affirm the natural character of the right to private ownership, including that of the means of production, while allowing for a large measure of public ownership of these.[20] Two years later, in 1963, *Pacem in Terris* included in its list of human rights that to private property, 'including the means of production'.[21] The Pope included this right among those held to be 'universal, inviolable and inalienable'.[22] This natural right has to be interpreted in an equivalent and virtual sense: it means a *personal* participation in control of the means of production, not necessarily possessing them as private property.

5. Vatican II: *Gaudium et Spes*

Gaudium et Spes, promulgated on 7 December 1965, makes an important affirmation: 'Human labour . . . is superior to the other elements of economic life. For the latter have only the nature of tools' (67a). This virtually contains a radical critique of capitalism, which has seen and still sees the rights of capital as foremost. *Gaudium et Spes* reaffirms the universal destination of land and all it contains to the community, for the use of every human being and people: 'Whatever the forms of ownership may be, as adapted to the legitimate institutions of people . . ., attention must always be paid to the universal purpose for which created goods are meant' (69a). On private property, it is notably cautious, free from any ideological dogmatization of the right to ownership (71b). What it says of ownership should be applied not only to material goods, but also to intangible ones, such as professional skills (71c).

So a long road in the social teaching of the church comes to an end: it started with the abstract anti-socialism of Leo XIII and has ended with a certain openness to a variety of (non-dogmatic) forms and possibilities of democratic socialism, taking account of the great variety of historical, social, economic and cultural situations that exist.

6. Paul VI: *Populorum Progressio*

This, on the subject of private property, follows the same line of thinking as *Gaudium et Spes*. One interesting contribution is its condemnation of the 'Manchester school' of free-market capitalism (26). In its day, this passage aroused a considerable amount of anger among capitalists and a degree of contempt from many liberal economists. The Pope is not issuing a blanket condemnation of the desire for economic profit, necessary for a dynamic economy, which is essential today for the survival and development of humankind. What he condemns, on moral grounds, is private, individualistic profit taken as an absolute end in itself, to which everything else must be subordinated: the idea that maximizing return on capital is the supreme value. Against this form of capitalism, *Populorum Progressio* reminds us that the economy is at the service of people.

7. John Paul II: *Laborem Exercens* and *Sollicitudo Rei Socialis*

The encyclical *Laborem Exercens* of 1981 deals systematically with the subject of human work. Its central thesis is this: work is the correct standpoint from which to focus critically on the whole social question (3b). Work is a basic dimension of human existence (4a). But work needs to be humanizing, a process of human self-fulfillment (4–6, 9). The structures of out-and-out capitalism are incompatible with the human significance of work (14d). Work displays the essential solidarity and social nature of personal human existence (12d, 13b, 14d).

Some critics have condemned this as an excessive absolutization of the 'metaphysics of work', which they see as outdated, preferring the intersubjectivity of *homo loquens* to the man-nature dialectic of *homo faber*. But the social valuation of work includes or conjugates both dialectics. *Laborem Exercens* refers to the nineteenth-century workers' movements for union and political rights in entirely positive terms (8b).

The encyclical *Sollicitudo Rei Socialis* of 1987 set out to bring the message of Paul VI's *Populorum Progressio* up to date, stating the need for a forceful affirmation of the possibility of genuinely human development and authentic liberation (47a). It maintains a certain neutrality between capitalism and collectivism, 'provided that the dignity of the human person is duly respected and promoted' (41b). Both systems are so imperfect that they stand in need of radical correction (21a).

The Pope vigorously denounces the bureaucratic centralism of collectivist economies (15b). In the face of the problems which this brings, he reaffirms the individual's right to economic initiative, going so far as to put this on a par with the right to religious freedom (15e, 42g). This seems excessive, particularly given the lack of analysis of what this 'initiative' might mean for every person in every situation within the complexity of the present economic systems and all their differing circumstances.

The encyclical proposes changes in the system of international trade, in the world monetary and financial system, and in the transfer of technology (43b-e). It argues for a greater degree of international control of all of these

(43g). 'Development,' it argues,' 'should be carried out within the framework of *solidarity* and *freedom*, without ever sacrificing one to the other under whatever pretext' (33h). John Paul II is not, however, envisaging the possibility of conflict between the two values, which leaves his statement somewhat up in the air. Vatican II's *Gaudium et Spes* (75d-e) is far more specific:

> The proper relationship between socialization on the one hand and personal independence and development on the other can be variously interpreted according to the locales in question and the degree of progress achieved by a given people. When the exercise of rights is temporarily curtailed on behalf of the common good, it should be restored as quickly as possible after the emergency passes. In any case it harms humanity when government takes on totalitarian or dictatorial forms injurious to the rights of persons or social groups.

Translated by Paul Burns

Notes

1. Cf.*Leonis XII Acta* XI, 1892, 100–2.
2. Cf. J. M. Díez-Alegría, *Cristianismo y propriedad privada*, Bilbao 1988, 11–68.
3. Cf. 1–2, q.94, a.5 ad 3; 2–2, q. 57, a. 3,c; q. 66, a. 2,cff.
4. Cf. *Acta* XI, 129–31.
5. Ibid., 102–3.
6. Ibid., 129–31.
7. Ibid., 133–5, 138–40.
8. Cf. AAS 23, 1931, 191.
9. Ibid., 204–6.
10. Ibid., 205.
11. Ibid., 200.
12. Cf. AAS 33, 1941, 199.
13. Loc. cit.
14. Cf. AAS 36, 1944, 252–3; 42, 1950, 485–7; 45, 1953, 37; 48, 1956, 30.
15. Cf encyclical *Sertum laetitiae*, 1 September 1939, in AAS 31, 1939, 643.
16. Radio address of 1 June 1941, in AAS 33, 1941, 201.
17. Cf. AAS 53, 1961, 426–7.
18. Ibid., 420.
19. Ibid., 423–4.
20. Ibid., 427–31.
21. Cf. AAS 55, 1963, 262.
22. Ibid., 259.

Socialism and Capitalism in Papal Social Teaching

Norbert Mette

*Dedicated to Professor Dr Ernst-Rüdiger Kiesow of Rostock
on his sixty-fifth birthday*

1. In place of socialism

The first official church statement on the social question in *Rerum Novarum* begins directly with an apologia for private property and thus goes on the defensive against the socialism of the time. Only with some reservations can this be described as a 'bad blemish', the words used by O. von Nell-Breuning in an attempt to tone it down.[1] A definitive condemnation of socialism or communism had in fact already been made on a number of occasions in previous papal declarations, beginning with the encyclical *Qui Pluribus* (1846), whose description of 'so-called communism' as a 'damnable doctrine which is already everywhere in conflict with natural law' was taken up by its author Pope Pius IX in his encyclical *Nostis et nobiscum* (1849) on the pastoral care of the churches (especially in Italy) in the face of socialism and communism and eventually endorsed summarily in the *Syllabus* (1864). This stance continued down to the encyclical *Quod Apostolici Muneris*, in which in the very first year of his pontificate (1878), Leo XIII attacked the 'deadly plague' of 'socialism, communism and nihilism'.

The following sentence from *Nostis et Nobiscum* is a good indication of the general tenor of these papal condemnations: 'It is certain that the teachers of both communism and socialism are pursuing the same goal, albeit with different means and methods, namely of deceiving the workers and other men of lowly state by lies and seducing them by the prospect of better living conditions, so as to spur them on to incessant revolt and gradually accustom them to increasingly serious crime, so that later with the help of their leaders they can fight against any higher authority, steal, rob and plunder the goods first of the church and then of all others, violate all divine and human rights, push religion aside, and destroy all the orders of bourgeois society' (17). This already sums up all the grounds on which from then on socialism was rejected by the *magisterium*: the stress on the equality of all men, the disputing of the right to private property, the destruction of marriage and the family, and the questioning of all social authority. This total attack on the foundations of society was ultimately derived from the denial of God and the natural and supernatural God-given order.

Leo XIII explicitly defended against this socialist doctrine the church's views of the divinely willed inequality of human beings in social matters (as opposed to their equality as children of God), and thus of the necessity of a hierarchical division of society; of the family as the origin of the state; and of the inviolability of private property. In order to combat the 'plague of socialism' he called for a development of the charitable institutions of the church and reminded the rich of their obligation 'to convey to the poor of their surplus' (*Quod Apostolici Muneris* 10). Finally, encouragement of the class-structured craftsmen's and workers' unions seemed to him an important response of socialist propaganda: 'these, founded under the protection of faith, induce in all members contentment with their lot and patience in their work, and lead them to a quiet, peaceful way of life' (12).

Against this background, the thesis that the specific occasion for the publication of the encyclical *Rerum Novarum* thirteen years later was the further advance of socialism cannot simply be rejected out of hand. Another pointer in this direction is that the first part of the encyclical begins with a refutation of the solutions proposed by socialism. However, it avoids once again sweepingly attributing all the ills of the present to 'socialism, communism and liberalism', and concentrates on identifying and rejecting the errors of the socialists on the property question. Even though talk of 'socialism' is still general, Leo XIII gives clear contours to what he means by this than in his earlier encyclicals. In particular it is noted that socialism is tainted with a concern in principle to abolish private property (RN 3).

A further point made is that socialism derives the necessity of the class struggle from the unreconciled opposition between capital and labour (15), that it dreams of a society in which there is no longer any social inequality (14), and that it wants to proceed with the introduction of universal state welfare for the family (11). In addition to some practical arguments, the main objection made by Leo XIII to this social programme is that it offends against basic principles of social order according to natural law and therefore can contribute nothing to the solving of the social question. Over against this he stresses as the beginnings of a strategy for social reform 'the demand for fair wages; the right of the workers to join together to protect their (legitimate) interests; and the obligation of the state to intervene in the economy (state intervention), if that is necessary to secure or sustain the common good'.[2]

It is clear that Leo XIII and his predecessors were dealing with a socialism (or what they regarded as socialism) which they encountered predominantly in programmatic form and which had only just begun to find expression in parties and their bonding together to form the Internationale. That situation had fundamentally changed forty years later, at the time when *Quadragesimo Anno* appeared. Since the October Revolution of 1919, Marxist-Leninist communism had become the formative principle of the society and economy of the USSR. In addition, the socialist alternative formed a more or less clear point of reference for the protest movement, fed by a variety of motives, against the capitalist economic system, the devastating social consequences of which were becoming increasingly clear. Though it was not expressed so strongly as in Protestantism, the thesis that in principle socialism and Christianity were compatible and indeed related had also found its advocates in the Catholic sphere.[3]

Pius XI reacted to this by noting the changes within socialism which had taken place since *Rerum Novarum* and distinguishing between a more acute trend, communism, and a more moderate trend (cf. QA 111ff.). Whereas he condemned communism unconditionally for its inhumanity and hostility to God, he conceded that the 'propaganda demands' of moderate socialism had a remarkable affinity to the 'postulates of a Christian social reform' (113). Thus for example he held that action against 'a social domination of the owner usurped contrary to all law', and action 'to withhold particular kinds of goods from the public hand' (114) was legitimate and compatible with the Christian view. The question is, however, whether such demands are in fact socialist at all.

For – and now Pius XII's argument changes from the historical-phenomenological level to the doctrinaire level of principles – the characteristic of socialism is that it does not know the 'exalted destiny of both human beings and society' which has been bestowed on them by God and sees society merely as a 'utilitarian organization' (118). To such an extent does the best possible provision of all the good things of earthly life seem the supreme good that 'unheedingly the highest human goods, not least their freedom, are sacrificed in total subjection to the material necessity of the absolutely rationalistic production of goods' (119).

Precisely for that reason socialism, even though it contains some true insights, 'always remains incompatible with the teaching of the Catholic church – it would have to cease to be socialism: the contrast between socialist and Christian views of society is unbridgable' (117; cf.also 120). Even if the understanding of socialism which underlies this statement goes back to a conceptuality constructed by G. Gundlach SJ,[4] so that – as later interpretations have brought out[5] – the conclusion expressed by the *magisterium* that Christianity and socialism are incompatible refers to socialism only in so far as it in fact displays the 'errors' mentioned, *Quadragesimo Anno* has widely been understood to have passed a verdict on socialism generally. For a long time the discussion about possible ways of collaboration with socialism or even of forms of Christian socialism was broken off in the Catholic sphere – a development was also influenced by the rise of Fascist rule in Europe. The condemnation of communism by the encyclical *Divini Redemptoris* (1937) of Pius XI intensified this further. And even Pius XII did not depart from the line laid down by his predecessors.[6]

It was not least through acquaintance with the political and social commitment of some Christians (e.g. in the British Labour Party or among the Social Democrats) who drew on the traditions of socialism, along with the rise of new forms of socialism in countries of the so-called 'Third World' which had been freed from colonial rule, and a new phase of theological grappling with these different trends, that the absolute verdict of the *magisterium* on socialism was gradually relaxed. The beginning of this was marked by John XXIII's encyclical *Mater et Magistra* (1961). While mentioning the verdict on socialism in *Quadragesimo Anno* (34), the encyclical does not endorse it once again. In the encyclical *Pacem in Terris* (1963), the same Pope made a distinction between 'those who are concerned with economic, social and cultural questions or with politics', and 'false philosophical views about the nature, origin and goal of the world and human beings'. Though these two may originally have belonged together, it has proved possible to separate them as a result of a historical process of change: the movement has in fact detached itself from its original doctrinal system and therefore there is no longer any obstacle in the way of collaborating with it (159).

Paul VI takes this up in his encyclical *Octogesima Adveniens* (1971, cf. 30), and comments on socialism, etc., as follows:

Distinctions must be made to guide concrete choices between the various levels of expression of socialism: a generous aspiration and a seeking for a more just society, historical movements with a political organization and aim; and an ideology which claims to give a complete and self-sufficient picture of man. Nevertheless, these distinctions must not lead one to consider such levels as completely separate and independent. The concrete line which, according to circumstances, exists between them, must be clearly marked out. This insight will enable Christians to see the degree of commitment possible along these lines, while safeguarding the values, especially those of liberty, responsibility and openness to the spiritual, which guarantee the integral development of man (31).

Granted, this does not say anything 'new' about socialism. But it does avoid summing up the various historical and regional forms under a single conceptual definition by means of which they are to be judged. Rather, the fact of multiplicity is accepted, and Christians are themselves made responsible for forming a judgment in the specific situation as to how far they may and should cooperate.[7]

The Pope is more restrained and adopts a generally warning tone over the possibilities of the partial reapproachment with Marxism which has been suggested by Christians (32–34). But he also distinguishes here between different notions of Marxism and does not *a priori* identify them with that 'Marxist ideology' to which he thinks it impossible for Christians to commit themselves.

'Socialism' no longer appears as an independent theme in the social encyclicals of Pope John-Paul II. *Laborem Exercens* (1981) still mentions 'scientific socialism', which is identified with the Marxist ideology. Its final goal is seen as the complete overthrow of the social order and the introduction of socialism and ultimately communism all over the world (11.4,5). In *Sollicitudo Rei Socialis* (1987), the Pope accuses both 'Marxist collectivism' and 'liberal capitalism' of being trapped in thinking in political and ideological blocks and of involvement in an increasing impoverishment of the nations, especially in the southern hemisphere, in their pursuit of power and profit (20ff.). Theologically both systems are to be branded 'structures' of sin and condemned (36f.). In particular, it is argued that 'Marxist collectivism' robs both individual citizens and whole nations of their autonomy and degrades them to become objects through its prevention of entrepreneurial initiative (15).

2. In place of capitalism

Some commentators on *Sollicitudo Rei Socialis* have been irritated that the present Pope passed equally negative verdicts on 'Marxist collectivism' and 'liberal capitalism' and postulated a critical attitude of the church towards them (21). They evidently have not been aware that the reservations about socialism to be found in papal social teaching do not mean that capitalism is generally justified. On the contrary, there have repeatedly been rejections of capitalism, the clarity of which leaves hardly anything to be desired. However, it is important to draw distinctions on this topic, too.

If the spread of socialism, especially among those who are impoverished and endlessly exploited, is really to be stopped, it is not enough to condemn it in merely theoretical terms; existing social abuses must also be removed. That is the position of Leo XIII. And with his plea for state intervention and associations for the effective representation of the workers' interest, he resolutely opposed the dominant liberal dogma of the capacity of the free market to regulate itself. He evidently believed that it had been proved on the basis of previous historical experience that the situation of the workers, which he sharply denounced (RN 1), could not be improved in this way. However, Leo XIII did not adopt the criticism of capitalism in principle which was then widespread in the Catholic church, but set out on his own course of social and political reform.

As Pius IX noted forty years later, the picture of the economy had changed completely (QA 100), and in his view the changes had been in a devastating direction. There were now the 'last repercussions of the spirit of individualism':

Free competition has destroyed itself; economic dictatorship has supplanted the free market; unbridled ambition for power has likewise succeeded greed for gain; all economic life has become tragically hard, inexorable and cruel. To these are to be added the grave evils that have resulted from an intermingling and shameful confusion of the functions and duties of public authority with those of the economic sphere . . . And as to international relations, two different streams have issued from the one fountain-head: On the one hand, economic nationalism or even economic imperialism; on the other, a no less deadly and accursed internationalism of finance or international imperialism whose country is where profit is . . . (109).

In a way which was extremely alien to many Catholics, since for them this was Marxist terminology, Pius XI also spoke of 'classes' and 'class struggle'. He stressed the need to remove the poison from the 'reprehensible class struggle' based on enmity and hatred in favour of an 'honest discussion between the classes prompted by a will for justice' (114).[8] We shall return to the question what model of social order he might possibly have had in mind.

However, a distinction must be made between this question and that of economic modes. In the judgment of Pius XI, in so far as the term 'capitalist' stresses that in general some provide the means of production and others the labour to achieve it in a shared concern', it is 'not intrinsically bad' (101). On the contrary, he credits this economic method with having improved the situation of the workers in developed countries (59). He also sees the positive side of free competition, as long as it is not elevated to be the supreme principle for ordering of society, and of contracts with workers, and affirms them both. The 'perverseness' only begins when these economic methods are combined with a liberal ideology and give free rein to interests dictated only by economics, without heed to the human dignity of the worker, without heed to the common good and common justice (101). Over against that, 'the principles of right reason . . . must be kept in mind in theory regarding ownership and labour and their association together, and must be put into actual practice' (110).

Pius XI's successors have maintained his distinction between the capitalist-style economy, which is regarded as value-neutral, and its ideological distortion. So on the one hand there is repeatedly the sharpest condemnation of 'capitalism'. (One example of this was the radio broadcast by Pius XII on 1 September 1944, in which he explicitly repudiated 'capitalism' because 'contrary to natural law' it was founded on erroneous conceptions and claimed an unlimited right 'to property without any subordination to the common good'.)[9] On the other hand it was maintained, as for example in *Populorum Progressio*, that this 'type of capitalism' is not simply to be identified with industrialization and the economic development which is moulded by it and blamed for everything. On the contrary, 'one must recognize in all justice the irreplaceable contribution made by the organization of labour and of industry to what development has accomplished' (26).

Pope John Paul II was the first to stop making this distinction. He uses the term 'capitalism' to denote a 'historically unique phenomenon', namely the socio-economic system 'as opposed to socialism and communism' (*Laborem Exercens* 7.3). This provisional definition is made more precise with the aid of a historical reconstruction which makes an instructive division of capitalism into phases.[10]

The characteristic of 'early capitalism' (LE 7,3) was to understand and treat work 'as a sort of "merchandise" that the worker – especially the industrial worker – sells to the employer, who at the same time is the possessor of the capital, that is to say, of all the working tools and means that make production possible' (7.2). Not least because of 'worker solidarity', this 'rigid capitalism' (14.4) has transformed itself into different forms of 'neo-capitalism' which would give a stronger legal status to work: 'Workers can often share in running businesses and in controlling their productivity, and in fact do so. Through appropriate associations, they exercise influence over conditions of work and pay, and also over social legislation' (8.4).

However, the Pope warns several times that the error of the 'period of primitive capitalism' (13.5), with its 'exclusive right to private ownership of the means of production' (14.4), has by no means been totally eradicated, and could therefore repeat itself (7.2,3; 13.5). Specifically, something of this kind could happen in the third phase of capitalism, which the Pope sees dawning as new technological, economic and political developments take place. As factors in the far-reaching changes which are associated with this, to an extent comparable to the industrial revolution of the previous century, he cites 'the widespread introduction of automation into many spheres of production, the increase in the cost of energy and raw materials, the growing realization that the heritage of nature is limited and that it is being intolerably polluted, and the emergence on the political scene of peoples who, after centuries of subjection, are demanding their rightful place among nations and in international decision-making' (1.3). Even if it need not come to this, the Pope sees a danger that in this third phase an 'economism and materialism' (13) will impose itself brutally and heedlessly. Unless it is resisted in solidarity, with its 'criterion of maximum profit' (17.4), it will bring 'other forms of injustice' which be far more wide-ranging than those of the previous century (8.4).

People in the so-called 'developing countries' are now affected by these ultimately fatal influences in a particularly gross form, seeing themselves the helpless victims of new forms of colonialism and imperialism:

> For instance the highly industrialized countries, and even more the businesses that direct on a large scale the means of industrial production (the companies referred to as multi-national or transnational), fix the highest possible prices for their products, while trying at the same time to fix the lowest possible prices for raw materials or semi-manufactured goods. This is one of the causes of an ever increasing disproportion between national incomes. The gap between most of the richest countries and the poorest ones is not diminishing or being stabilized but is increasing more and more, to the detriment, obviously, of the poor countries (17.3).[11]

3. A 'third way'?

The clear reserve towards both the socialist and the capitalist systems has increasingly suggested that papal social teaching is pleading for a 'third way' – to some degree between socialism and capitalism. Indeed there are indications of this: in the early declarations of the *magisterium*, socialism is seen less in contrast to capitalism than as being a kind of liberalism.[12] And it is this liberalism which is made responsible for all the misery of the social question, because it destroys the way society is ordered into classes and thus has undermined the 'Christian spirit'. So it is not surprising that in nineteenth-century Catholicism there was a widespread idea that only a restoration of the corporate state ordered by classes could lead to a real solution of the social question.[13]

Though not in the strictly anti-capitalist variant of, say, the Vogelsang school, this view can also be found in Leo XIII. 'Though this is not said in so many words, the whole context indicates that in Leo's view society is composed of a stratum of those who are "born" well-to-do and a stratum of those who are "born" with fewer possessions, who through their lack of possessions are forced into unpopular jobs which are nevertheless indispensable to society.'[14] So the issue is to help the workers to their due 'state' and give proper material and notional support to this place in society which is their due.

The axiom stressed in *Rerum Novarum* and continually repeated since then, that 'there can be no capital without labour, nor labour without capital' (15), corresponds to this. Instead of the transcending of the antagonism of capital and labour in the class-*less* society, there is thus a plea that this contrast should be transplanted to become a flourishing collaboration between the two in a class-*free* society – though this will not be devoid of conflict.[15] This view found its clearest – and at the same time most controversial – expression in the model of the 'class order' conceived by Pius XI (QA 76–98): it may have been influenced by Heinrich Pesch SJ's concept of solidarity,[16] but shows an affinity to contemporary Fascist notions of society which can hardly be disputed.[17]

It is no coincidence that such ideas of social order had no effect. On the one hand their categories were inappropriate to actual social developments, and on the other mere calls for a 'reform of disposition' were incapable of putting a stop to this development.

It was therefore only logical for Pope John-Paul II expressly to reject ideas of a 'third way':

The Church's social doctrine is not a 'third way' between liberal capitalism and Marxist collectivism, nor even a possible alternative to other solutions less radically opposed to one another; rather, it constitutes a category of its own. Nor is it an ideology, but rather the accurate formulation of the results of a careful reflection on the complex realities of human existence, in society and in the international order, in the light of faith and of the church's tradition. Its main aim is to interpret these realities, determining their conformity with or divergence from the lines of the Gospel teaching on man and his vocation, a vocation which is both earthly and transcendent; its aim is thus to guide Christian behaviour (SRS 41).

In conclusion, the following comments may be made on the claim which papal social teaching itself thus makes:

1. Even if church social teaching does not want to be an ideology, there can be no disputing that it is often claimed to be one. It has itself contributed considerably to this situation in that for a long time nineteenth-century statements of papal teaching began with a discussion on an ideological level before – at a late stage – getting to grips with the social question. Moreover, the papal attitude to socialism and capitalism proved to be conceptually so enigmatic that it even prompted opposed interpretations.[18]

2. The fact is that if papal social teaching had any historical influence at all, this was at most on the formation of capitalist societies, in that with the help of social and political reform measures, the parties and associations shaped by it committed themselves to a gradual transformation of 'hard (Manchester) capitalism' into a 'socially tempered capitalism'. So for the socialists, church social teaching undeniably belonged to the 'opposite camp'. Conversely, the arguments from the Catholic church against socialism long remained inadequate.[19] It was left to the initiatives of individual church 'outsiders' to pioneer that differentiated perspective on socialism which Paul VI finally recognized.[20]

3. One significant change in papal social teaching has been the way in which – after *Populorum Progressio* – it has increasingly taken into account the experiences of individuals and countries who find themselves on what Gustavio Gutíerrez has called the 'underside of history' – the impoverished and oppressed, particularly in the southern hemisphere – and has called for their comprehensive liberation.[21] In the new phase of an increasingly heedless 'thoroughgoing capitalization' of all social spheres and forms of interpersonal life, one particular, much-needed contribution of church social teaching would be unswervingly to bring to bear the biblical 'preferential option for the poor', allied with practical commitment to the dignity of all human beings and to social justice.[22] All this, however,

presupposes that the church and Christians are ready self-critically to concede and remedy their own entanglements in the capitalist system and thus in the 'structures of sin'.

Translated by John Bowden

Notes

1. O. von Nell-Breuning, *Soziallehre der Kirche. Erläuterungen der lehramtlichen Dokumente*, Vienna 1977, 33.
2. W. Kroh, *Kirche im gesellschaftlichen Widerspruch*, Munich 1982, 44.
3. Cf. F. Focke, *Sozialismus aus christlicher Verantwortung*, Wuppertal [2]1981.
4. Cf. G. Gundlach, 'Sozialismus', *Staatslexikon* 4, Freiburg [5]1931, 1688–96, esp.1693; cf. J. Schwarte, *Gustav Gundlach SJ (1892–1963). Massgeblicher Repräsentant der katholischen Soziallehre während der Pontifikate Pius' XI and Pius' XII*, Paderborn 1975, esp.419–28.
5. Cf. F. Klüber, *Katholische Soziallehre und demokratischer Sozialismus*, 'Der Kampf um die soziale Gerechtigkeit in Vergangenheit und Gegenwart', in id., *Den Kapitalismus umbiegen*, ed. F. Hengsbach et al., Düsseldorf 1990, 171–87, esp.181–4.
6. Cf. F. Klüber, *Katholische Gesellschaftslehre*, Vol.1, Osnabrück 1968, 332–78.
7. Cf. S. H. Pfürtner and W. Heierle, *Einführung in die katholische Soziallehre*, Darmstadt 1980, 112.
8. Cf. O. von Nell-Breuning, 'Katholische Kirche und Marxsche Kapitalismuskritik', in id., *Kapitalismus* (n.5), 197–207; R. Weiler, 'Catholic Social Teaching and the Class Struggle in the German Language Countries', *Concilium* 105, 1977, 50–77; K. Füssel, 'Theoretical Aspects of Class Struggle', ibid., 58–64.
9. Quoted from Klüber, *Katholische Soziallehre* (n.5), 366f.
10. Cf. G. Baum, *The Priority of Labour*, New York 1982.
11. Cf. in more detail *Sollicitudo Rei Socialis*.
12. According to W. E. von Ketteler, liberalism is the 'father of socialism', cf. E. Iserloh, 'Wilhelm Emmanuel von Ketteler und die Freiheit der Kirche und in der Kirche', in *Texte zur katholischen Soziallehre* III, Kevelaer 1978, 293–319.
13. Cf. Kroh, *Kirche* (n.2), 21–57; cf. also B. Casper, '"Sozialismus" im Sprachgebrauch der römische Kurie um 1850', in A. Langener, *Katholizismus, konservative Kapitalismuskritik und Frühsozialismus bis 1850*, Munich, etc. 1975, 194–206.
14. O. von Nell-Breuning, 'Standwerdung der Arbeiterschaft?', in I. Brusis and M. Grönefelt (ed.), *Unbequeme Grenzziehung*, Cologne 1990, 91–8: 96.
15. Cf. id., 'Katholische Kirche' (n.5), 205.
16. Cf. A. Rauscher, 'Solidarismus', in id. (ed.), *Der soziale und politische Katholizismus*, Vol.1, Munich 1981, 340–68.
17. For a summary see Klüber, *Katholische Soziallehre* (n.5), 309–15.
18. See the article on 'Catholic Social Teaching in Germany between Competing Trends', below 65–82.
19. Cf. *Anti-Sozialismus aus Tradition? Memorandum des Bensberger Kreises zum Verhältnis von Christentum und Sozialismus heute*, Reinbek 1976.
20. Cf. Focke, *Sozialismus* (n.3).

21. Cf. in detail *Sollicitudo Rei Socialis*.

22. Cf. D. Door, *Option for the Poor. A Hundred Years of Vatican Social Teaching*, Maryknoll 1983.

Theological Categories in the Social Encyclicals

John A. Gallagher

The centenary of the publication of Leo XIII's *Rerum Novarum* is an opportune occasion to reflect upon a very specific theological genre which has become a major component of the Catholic theological heritage. The papal encyclical tradition, of which the social encyclicals have become the most widely read and commented-upon segment, is a theological genre which can be defined in terms of its authorship, audience and purpose. As instruments of papal teaching office, the encyclicals have always enjoyed a privileged position which has distinguished them within the Catholic theological heritage. Vatican I's decree on papal infallibility as well as the Council's overall ecclesiology significantly enhanced the significance to be attributed to documents of papal authorship. As letters addressed to the whole church, and in most cases implicitly, if not explicitly, 'to all men of good will', the encyclicals have attempted to reach the minds and hearts of the entire Catholic episcopacy, the laity throughout the world, and all persons seeking to live a full and complete human existence. The persistent purpose of this theological genre has been to call members of the church and all who would hear the voice of the Holy See to a set of proper beliefs and to a way of life consistent with God's providential ordering of the world through the works of creation and redemption. The encyclical tradition has sought to provide a foundational theology which could sustain an authentic Catholic way of life amidst the opportunities and dangers of modern culture.

The encyclical as a theological genre is undoubtedly an outgrowth of the epistolary components of the New Testament and the mediaeval decretalist tradition. In both instances persons specifically charged with the spiritual well-being of Christian communities attempted to provide guidance and leadership to counteract forces internal or external to the church which threatened either its orthodoxy or its orthopraxis. Both types of writings were letters of guidance, instruction and exhortation to a way of life consistent with the gospel. What distinguishes the modern encyclical genre from its earlier paradigms, at least in part, is its universality. Papal encyclicals are addressed not to the unique needs of a local church, but rather to questions and issues which pose problems to the church universal, problems which are usually viewed as affecting the social and cultural conditions in which persons pursue the purpose of their creation, authentic human existence as a means to union with God.

The genre of the encyclical has been a voice within the Catholic theological heritage which has co-existed with other theological genres. The papal encyclicals can be clearly distinguished from the neo-Thomist manuals of seminary theology, just as they can be distinguished from the historical theologies of Congar and Daniélou, from Latin-American, African and feminist liberation theologies, from the transcendental theologies of Rahner or Lonergan, or from the political theology of Metz. The genre of the encyclical has shared the theological stage with other protagonists which have jointly created the drama of Catholic theology. It has collaborated with theological genres (neo-Thomism, neo-scholasticism), and condemned others (the historicism of Loisy and the *nouvelle théologie*). Thus, although the papal encyclical tradition is a discrete, identifiable theological genre, its exhortations and repudiations bear witness to the fact that it has co-existed with and scripted its self-understanding in relation to a wider theological heritage of which it is a part. The primary concern of the social encyclicals has been pastoral, practical and foundational theology, not speculative, systematic theology.

The genre of papal encyclicals has also defined itself in relation to non-theological movements. Kantian philosophy, socialism, liberalism, communism and existentialism have each evoked a response from the papal tradition. In its encyclical letters, the papacy has attempted to respond to signs of the times, occurrences in the process of human development, and especially social and economic theories which would direct that development in directions incompatible with papal theology.

The encyclical genre which has been developed by the papacy between 1891 and 1991 can be defined in terms of its authorship, its audience and its purpose. The content and the specific positions which this genre have explicitly enunciated have largely been articulated in response to theological, intellectual, social, economic and political movements of the past century. The encyclical genre can be yet further defined in terms of its internal constitutive elements. Among the essential constitutive elements of the genre have been the natural law and the law of grace, reason and faith, and a conception of the ultimate purpose of human existence. As a play or novel requires plot and dénouement, as poetry requires versification, so papal encyclicals (most especially the social encyclicals) have been the result of the creative interplay between the dynamics of these defining characteristics of the genre and competing views of the grounds of human authenticity.

The present study will investigate two of these constitutive elements of the social encyclicals : the natural law and the law of grace. These two themes, which are essential to the warp and woof of the social encyclicals, will first be examined as instances of what Bernard Lonergan has referred to as general and special theological categories. Then, the manner in which each category has been specified and developed over the course of one hundred years of papal reflection will be assessed. Finally, the dynamic and changing relationship between these categories will provide evidence of a fundamental reorientation within the encyclical tradition.

1. Theological categories

Categories attempt to determine the transcendent reality which is the ultimate object of theology. In one manner or another Catholic theology has been an effort first, to describe God and the divine nature, and then, second, to interpret the meaning and significance of God's activity towards the world. St Thomas, for instance, first posed the question of the existence of God and then reflected upon the divine nature and its attributes. Only after he had examined the question of God *in se* did he direct his attention to the doctrines of creation and providence in order to elaborate his understanding of the meaning and signficance of God's activity in regard to the world. But like all great Christian theologians, Thomas was aware that it was impossible to describe God as such or adequately to portray the gracious activity of God in the world. All that the student of the divine can hope to achieve is a more or less fitting portrayal in human (analogical or metaphorical) language of the transcendent reality which is the object of theological inquiry. Theological categories are the analogical or metaphorical expressions of the acts of understanding produced by theological investigation.

Bernard Lonergan has distinguished between general and special theological categories.[1] General theological categories relate to objects that come within the purview of theology as well as other disciplines. When theologians speak of three *persons* in one God, when they attribute *sonship* to Jesus, when the term *redemption* is employed to describe what the Son of God accomplished for humanity, terms drawn from human experience or terms developed in theoretical interpretations of human experience are used to describe the divine or divine activity. These are categories or terms drawn from the realm of human endeavours, which are used analogically to describe certain characteristics of God. To the Father, the Son and the Holy Spirit are attributed characteristics associated with *personhood*. But clearly each of the divine persons is a person in a manner which is ultimately more unlike than like the personhood of human beings. What term, what category, might be employed which would more adequately describe what there are three of in God? General theological categories are analogies drawn from the realm of human experience which enable theologians in a very limited manner to depict the divine reality and its action towards the world. The meaning of these terms generally receive their significance, their range of connotation and denotation from their usage among men and women. These words are then used to make concrete the attempts of theologians to describe the transcendent reality of God.

Special theological categories 'regard the objects proper to theology'.[2] The connotation and denotation associated with terms such as *God*, *grace*, *Trinity* pertain directly to the specifically religious dimension of human experience. Special theological categories have as their prime reference the divine reality itself. If these categories take on meaning within general parlance, with terms such as *gracious* the prime analogue is the divine activity. Both general and special theological categories strive to make concrete the human experience of the divine. General theological categories do so by drawing upon terms used elsewhere in human discourse; special theological categories represent the language developed to describe directly the transcendent openness of religious experience.

The importance of general and special theological categories is not limited to their making humanity's appropriation of the transcendent referent of its religiosity concrete. Terms, categories and words have a very 'bare bones' meaning until they are joined to the flesh and sinew of sentences, paragraphs and whole stories to form discourse. Theological categories, Lonergan has proposed, 'will form a set of interlocking terms and relations and, accordingly, they will possess the utility of models'.[3] Such models and discourses bring together general and special theological categories in a manner that makes possible a relatively adequate portrayal of the religious dimension of human experience and its interaction with other such dimensions.[4] Theology is not just the assertion of religious or theological terms, but rather the conscious effort to articulate and interpret them in a manner that enlightens the human experience of contemporary men and women. Such categories and the discourse they engender sustain and create the realm of meaning, the truly human world in which persons seek to discover, and to live in accord with, their authentic humanity.

The natural law and the law of grace are two particular instances of general and special theological categories. Both categories refer to the divine ordering of the moral universe. Natural law in all of the many understandings attributed to it in the course of Western thought has at least this one common feature: there are moral duties incumbent upon men and women which arise from their specifically human endowment. What that specifically human endowment consists of has been the object of humanistic investigation since the rise of culture. Over the centuries of Christian thought various interpretations, or at least distinct emphases, have been attributed to the natural law as the result of changing and developing humanistic studies in the wider culture. The issue of a just wage, for instance, only became an important issue for natural-law theorists when industrialization replaced agriculture as the dominant economic enterprise in the West. The discussion and interaction between theologians and other researchers into the authentically human creates a discourse of meaning in which human life can be lived in a truly human manner. Natural law is an instance of a general theological category which draws upon conceptions of the authentically human as developed in non-theological investigations to articulate the divine ordering of the moral universe.

The law of grace is a special theological category which draws directly upon the transcendent openness of human experience, and the manner in which this has been mediated through scripture to describe the divine ordering of the moral universe. Catholicism, and the Christian tradition generally, has insisted upon the doctrines of creation and redemption as central theological categories for any adequate interpretation of the specifically human. The law of grace, which encompasses both the Old and the New Laws, is the theological category which depicts the ongoing, active continuation of God's directing of human life. It is the indwelling of the Holy Spirit. As a decisive instance of divine providence, the law of grace refers to the manner in which God continues to be active and supportive of humanity's search for its meaning and purpose. The demands of the law of grace are experienced in humanity's continuing experience of the call to conversion, to *metanoia*, to an awareness of the fragility and incompleteness of human achievements, the abiding invitation arising from the religiosity of persons to a more profound holiness and goodness. The law of grace joins in the discourse of the natural law and humanistic studies to assert the profoundly religious dimension of human authenticity. Apart from religion there can be no authentic humanity. In the words of St Augustine, 'Our hearts are restless until they rest in thee.'

2. The natural law and the law of grace in the social encyclicals

A basic concern of the papal social encyclicals has been to present an interpretation of authentic human existence which was thought superior to the suggestions proposed by either liberalism or socialism. In creating the genre of the social encyclicals, the Popes entered upon a form of discourse which drew heavily upon both the natural law and the law of grace as theological categories. As Calvez and Perrin have commented, these categories were employed as 'two sources of social teaching which were placed side by side'.[5] I believe that it can be said that the law of grace and the natural law constituted the dominant categories which controlled this discourse.

Throughout the social encyclicals, the Popes repeatedly refer to the relevance of the natural law and the law of grace for any adequate construal of the moral universe. In *Graves de Communi*, Leo XIII encouraged his readers not to 'condemn the zeal which according to natural and divine law has this for its object, viz., to make the conditions of those who toil more tolerable'.[6] Paul VI reflected the same attention to the relevance of these two categories for an adequate interpretation of the moral order when he proposed that human problems need to be addressed in the light of an 'integral vision of man and his vocation, not only his natural and earthly, but also his supernatural and eternal vocation'.[7] 'The future,' Pius XII warned his readers on the eve of World War II, 'must rest on the solid rock of the natural law and of divine revelation'.[8] Examples of the Popes referring to both categories, and thus inferring the importance of the relationship (discourse) between them as essential for a portrayal of the authentically human, recur throughout the genre. But what did the Popes mean by these two terms?

A. *Natural law*

As was stated above, the social encyclicals have emerged from the pastoral, practical and foundational concerns of the papacy. Thus it is not surprising that one does not find theoretical or systematic attempts to define or even to clarify a category such as *natural law*. The denotations and connotations which the Popes have associated with this category must be construed from the literary contexts in which it has been employed. A cursory examination of these contexts, which is all that can be attempted here, reveals a significant shift in the referent of this category.

In the writings of Leo XIII, Pius XI and Pius XII the natural law is presented in what is probably its classic Catholic expression. The natural law is construed as a metaphysical characteristic of human nature which is the prime source of the normatively human. The equality among persons, Leo XIII wrote, 'consists in this: that all, having inherited the same nature, are called to the same most high dignity of the sons of God; and one and the same end is set before all, each of which is to be judged by the same law and will receive the same punishment or reward according to his deserts'.[9] According to Leo XIII, the natural law ought to govern the acts of individual men in their living out of their destiny. The same law ought also to govern the relations between classes of persons, especially that between workers and capitalists, whom nature has ordained 'should exist in harmony and agreement'.[10] The capacity of human nature to establish the basis of the moral order was most clearly asserted with regard to human sexuality. *Casti Connubii*'s condemnation of contraception asserted that 'no reason, however grave, can be put forward by which anything intrinsically against nature may become conformable to nature and the morally good'.[11]

This classical understanding of the natural law has its counterpart in the neo-Thomist manuals of moral theology.[12] Both the Popes and the manualists strove to provide their readers with accurate interpretations of St Thomas's natural-law theory. The natural law was thus construed to be a metaphysical ordering of human reality, biological and social, which created the environment in which human life could be meaningfully and purposefully lived. God's moral ordering of the world provided the standards by which true instances of authentic human flourishing could be detected as the fitting means to human nature's ultimate finality in God. Because this ordering was developed in metaphysical categories, it was thought to be invariable over time and between cultures.

Perhaps with Pius XII's elevation of the notion of human dignity to greater centrality in papal social thought, but certainly in the encyclicals of John XXIII, Paul VI, and most recently John Paul II, a new set of meanings seem to replacing those associated with classical natural-law theory. In his 1944 Christmas address, Pius XII reflected upon the human disaster resulting from World War II. The resulting danger, he proposed, was an abdication of human dignity. But it was in the name of human dignity that persons were calling out for more democratic forms of government.[13] From this point on in the development of papal social thought human dignity increasingly supplants human nature as the basic standard of justice (note that this does not apply to any aspect of sexual morality).

Leo XIII and Pius XI were attentive to the manner in which social conditions affected the specific manner in which human goods could be pursued and obtained. But as human dignity has become the central referent of papal natural-law theory, even greater importance has been attached to the social and cultural conditions which contextualize the quest for human authenticity. Given these developments, it is hardly surprising that the historical facet of moral norms has been given increasing significance.

John XXIII's *Mater et Magister* was a major impetus in the development of this new line of papal thought. Pope John construed the common good as 'the sum total of those conditions of social living whereby men are enabled more fully and readily to achieve their own perfection'.[14] Questions of justice, he continued, ought not be restricted to the distribution of wealth, but should be extended 'to the conditions under which men engage in productive activity'.[15] The human responsibility for which contemporary persons are accountable accords 'not merely with the nature of man, but also is in conformity with historical developments in the economic, social and political fields'.[16] Pope John seems to have been proposing that the cultural and social structures which human beings create in order to foster their pursuit of authenticity are themselves the source of relevant moral norms.

The same theme was emphasized in the social encyclicals of Paul VI. The development of peoples had become an issue of growing interest to the church, the activities of those who were looking for a 'wider share in the benefits of civilization and a more active improvement of their human qualities'.[17] Such development, however, must be integral; it must promote the good of every person and of the whole person.[18] Such a true humanism which promotes and enhances the human well-being of societies and individuals serves as a new referent for the natural law. The language and the nature of the discourse it invites reflects a concern to include the humanistic and social sciences as sources for determining specific moral requirements stemming from this new humanism.

In *Redemptor Hominis*, John Paul II queried whether the notion of human progress, 'which has man for its author and promoter, makes life on earth more human in every aspect of that life. Does it make a more worthy man?'[19] The writings of John Paul II contain a hermeneutic of suspicion concerning the course of recent human history. In a subsequent encyclical, he spoke of the present solicitude for the welfare of persons as not a matter of giving an abstract answer to who man is. He has no interest in returning to a metaphysical reading of human nature, but rather insists that the process of historical development be viewed as 'a matter of the whole dynamism of life and civilization . . . a matter of meaningfulness'.[20] The Pope is sceptical of discourses concerning human meaningfulness which are confined to natural-law categories, i.e. to 'premises given by man's own experience, his reason, and his sense of human dignity'.[21] To what, then, would he direct our attention?

B. *The law of grace*

The law of grace as a special theological category was regularly referred to in the social encyclicals prior to John Paul II. Its referent in some contexts was the law of the Old or New Testaments; in other contexts, its referent was the virtue of charity. Throughout this literature there is a constant attentiveness to God's ordering of the moral universe in a manner not comprehended by the natural law. An adequate comprehension of the moral universe should not restrict its vision to the realm of divine immanence, but ought to remain open to the significance of human transcendence, human religiosity.

If previous papacies have placed greater reliance on the natural law as a source for moral norms to guide humankind's quest for its meaning and purpose, then clearly a mark of the present papacy has been its emphasis on the law of grace as the primary theological category which ought to guide human and Christian life. This conviction of John Paul II has taken several courses.

Scripture has always played a decisive role in arriving at contemporary Christian moral norms. In the social encyclicals the scriptures are generally employed in a scholastic manner. Differences or tensions between scriptural citations are reconciled into meaningful moral norms. Scripture was also employed for paraenetic purposes in order to exhort persons to a life of virtue. Thus scripture was used as a medium by which the Holy Spirit enters the minds and hearts of Christians to make possible and to facilitate a life congruent with humanity's finality of union with God. For John Paul II the scriptures have become a more immediate source for the meaningfulness and purposefulness of human life. *Dives et Misericordia* and *Laborem Exercens* are fundamentally exegeses of the Old and New Testaments. The Pope turns directly to scripture and its interpretation as the source of categories descriptive of human well-being, rather than to some interpretation of the natural law. His theology offers a fundamentally new understanding of these two theological categories and their interrelationship.

If there were a precedent in previous papal social thought for this development in the theology of John Paul II, it might well be found in Paul VI. In *Octogesima Adveniens* Paul VI described:

The Spirit of the Lord, who animates men renewed in Christ, continually breaks down the horizons within which his understanding likes to find security and the limits to which his activity would willingly restrict itself; there dwells within him a power which urges him to go beyond every system and every ideology. As the heart of the world there dwells the mystery of man discovering himself to be God's son in the course of a historical and pyschological process in which constraint and freedom as well as the weight of sin and the breath of the spirit alternate and struggle for the upper hand.[22]

In Paul VI, and now much more clearly and pervasively in John Paul II, the law of grace becomes the criterion by which human progress must be assessed and necessarily found wanting. This perspective engenders a suspicious and reticent attitude toward any pretensions of human achievement or progress. Since the law of grace as a special theological category draws its primary referent directly from the transcendent dimension of human experience, it is difficult to criticize its claims to human significance from the perspective of the more immanent dimensions of human experience.

3. Conclusion

For the one hundred years of modern papal social theology, both the natural law and the law of grace have played formidable roles in the shaping of that discourse. A not infrequent critique of Catholic social ethics, both that of the manuals and that of the social encyclicals, has been that they were excessively reliant on rigid, naturalistic interpretations of the natural law. In the writings of the present Pope the pendulum seems to have swung to the other side. Will the sort of social theology so heavily dependent upon the law of grace provide a more adequate *religious* ethic? Will this type of theological ethic be capable of entering into meaningful discourse with humanistic scholars? Will the sharp dichotomy between the secular and the religious to which such an ethic attempts to respond be sharpened or mitigated by this type of theology? These are among the questions that remain to be answered.

Notes

1. Bernard Lonergan, *Method In Theology*, London and New York 1972, 282.
2. Ibid.
3. Ibid., 285.
4. See, for instance, John E. Smith, *Experience and God*, New Haven 1968, esp. 3–67.
5. Jean Calvez and Ives Perrin, *The Church and Social Justice*, London 1961, 39.
6. Leo XIII, *Graves de Communi*, in Joseph Husslein, *Social Wellsprings* (2 vols), Milwaukee 1940–42, Vol 1, 234.

7. Paul IV, *Humanae Vitae*, in Joseph Gremillion, *The Gospel of Peace and Justice*, Maryknoll 1976,430.
8. Pius XII, *Summi Pontificatu*, New York nd, 23.
9. Leo XIII, *Quod Apostolici Muneris*, in Social Wellsprings, Vol. 1, 18.
10. Leo XIII, *Rerum Novarum*, in *Social Wellsprings*, Vol. 1, 177.
11. Pius XI, *Casti Connubii*, in *Social Wellsprings*, Vol. 2, 143.
12. John A. Gallagher, *Time Past, Time Future*, New York 1990, 84–93.
13. Pius XII, 'Christmas Message – 1944', in *Pius XII and Democracy*, New York 1945, 301.
14. John XXIII, *Mater et Magister*, in *The Gospel of Peace and Justice*, 157.
15. Ibid., 161.
16. Ibid., 163.
17. Paul VI, *Populorum Progressio*, in *The Gospel of Peace and Justice*, 387.
18. Ibid., 391–2.
19. John Paul II, *Redemptor Hominis*, in *Origins* 8, 1979, 643.
20. Ibid., 635.
21. Ibid., 637.
22. Paul VI, *Octogesima Adveniens*, in *The Gospel of Peace and Justice*, 502.

The Ideological Uses of Catholic Social Teaching

Michael J. Schuck

From one standpoint, investigating the ideological uses of 'official' Catholic social teaching implies that the papal, conciliar and episcopal documents have been developed and employed less to promote social justice than to preserve the power interests of the Roman Catholic church. But the concept of 'ideology' is multiform. Thus, calling social teaching 'ideological' invites analysis from more than one standpoint.

The present article differentiates various meanings of ideology and identifies what each reveals about the ideological uses of Catholic social teaching. It then analyses the church's 'official' interpretation of ideology and concludes with an argument supporting the application of the concept to the social teaching of the church.

The concept of 'ideology'

Several meanings are assigned to the concept 'ideology' in contemporary humanities and social science literature. Some authors use the term pejoratively, defining ideology as a set of beliefs which serve to mask truth. Others interpret ideology in a non-pejorative way, construing it as a set of beliefs articulated to advance truth. Both these understandings have subdivisions. Some 'pejorativists' think that ideologies mask social interests; others believe they conceal social strains. Some 'non-pejorativists' equate ideology with any comprehensive system of social ideas; others with strategies for social action. Each approach requires brief elaboration.

A classic statement of the view that ideologies mask social interests occurs in Part One of Marx and Engels' *The German Ideology*. Because 'the ideas of the ruling class are in every epoch the ruling ideas', Marx and Engels argue that the 'ideas of those who lack the means of mental production are subject to [them]'.[1] In this way the powerful blind the powerless to the source of their oppression. An ideology, then, is a deliberate distortion of the truth, a disguise for the social interests of those in power.

The theory that ideologies conceal social strain draws on the work of Freud and Durkheim and is exemplified in Talcott Parsons' *The Social System*. According to Parsons, 'integration of the social system is the primary function of its common ideology'. 'Where there is an element of malintegration in the actual social structure,' he continues, 'the tendency will be for the ideology to gloss it over and play it down.'[2] In this view, ideologies function as therapeutic responses to disruptive social change. Though not a deliberate distortion of truth, an ideology provides an illusion of order which temporarily relieves social strain and forestalls confrontation with reality.

Those who think that an ideology is any system of social ideas are indebted to Theodor Geiger's *Ideology and Truth* and, more recently, Clifford Geertz's *The Interpretation of Cultures*. Ideologies, Geertz argues, are 'schematic images of social order', 'templates for the organization of social and psychological processes'.[3] This non-pejorative approach makes ideology synonymous with 'world-view': a body of connected ideas about society and humanity rooted in an individual's or group's reflective quest for truth.

The notion that an ideology is less a set of inert ideas than a catalyst for social action recalls DeStutt de Tracy's original use of the term in eighteenth-century France. As one of the Enlightenment 'idéologistes', Tracy analysed human ideas to eradicate bias and build a rational, scientific and liberal society. Though Karl Marx rarely used the term in this way, he reflected Tracy's intention in observing that 'philosophers have only "interpreted" the world . . . the point is to "change" it'.[4] From this perspective, ideologies serve not to mask truth, but advance it – and advance it not by ideation, but action.

These four approaches do not cover all the nuances given to the concept of ideology in current humanities and social science literature. They do, however, represent the broad lines of contemporary understanding, lines which have – in fact – been employed in the analysis and judgment of Catholic social teaching.

Ideology and Catholic social teaching

When commentators suggest that the 'official' social teaching of the Roman Catholic church has been put to ideological use they can mean one, or a combination, of the following: it has masked social interests, concealed social strain, presented social ideas, or generated social action. This section gives examples of how each approach has been employed in the commentary literature.

Some analysts argue that the prime motive behind Catholic social teaching has not been the advancement of truth, but the protection of church interests in society. This understanding is used as either a total or partial explanation of the church documents.

In *Liberalism and Its Critics*, Renzo Bianchi takes the total position that Catholic social teaching is a mask for church interests. His assessment of Leo XIII's *Rerum Novarum* is illustrative. After studying the Pope's 'bewildering maze of naive anthropology and social psychology, economic contradictions and anachronistic sociology', Bianchi concludes that it is 'difficult to avoid the impression that all this confusion' was 'designed'. But designed for what? Like the texts that succeed it, *Rerum Novarum* protected the ruling groups 'upon whose good will much of the power of the Church rested'.[5] It did this by appeasing working-class Catholics with abstract criticism of the rich and stigmatizing their participation in any potentially disruptive social movements. For Bianchi, then, the underlying concern of the papal social documents is institutional protection and power.

Marie-Dominique Chenu accepts this interpretation in part. Prior to the Second Vatican Council, the institutional church responded to social problems with answers deduced from abstract principles. Though ostensibly created to defend the powerless, this 'monolithic and universalisable "doctrine"' actually served 'as an ideological sanction for those who hold economic and political power and want to maintain the *status quo*'.[6] Postconciliar documents such as Paul VI's *Octagesima Adveniens* recognized this problem and encouraged a more inductive method, one motivated by a gospel-inspired reading of the 'signs of the times'. This new perspective is also suggested by the increased use of the phrase 'social teaching', rather than 'social doctrines', among church officials. But the latter phrase still resurfaces, meaning that the temptation to make Catholic social teaching an ideological mask for church interests endures.[7]

Paul Lakeland is less interested in how social teaching masks church interests than in how it conceals social strains. In his view, Catholic social teaching retains a vestige of the pre-conciliar church's 'serious fears and deep lack of confidence' concerning the modern world.[8] This shows in its persistent attachment to a 'premodern world-view'. With this world-view, Catholic social teaching shuns modern methods of reflexive (or self-) criticism. Instead, it seriously entertains only those ideas which already fit within an acceptable 'preordained ideological position'. Similarly, church teaching skirts the modern desideratum of open, undominated discourse by granting 'epistemologically exempt status' (or unquestioned validity) to the ideas of institutional officials.[9] In other words, 'official' social thought assumes an ecclesiology which systematically conceals deep tensions between the church and the modern world. For Lakeland, the ideological use of Catholic social teaching is more a matter of uncritical response to social strain than deliberate distortion of truth.

Unlike Bianchi, Chenu and Lakeland, some students of Catholic social teaching use the concept 'ideology' non-pejoratively. In this way, church teaching may be interpreted as either offering a world-view or motivating human action.

One of the first non-pejorative descriptions of Catholic social teaching as an ideology is Richard L. Camp's *The Papal Ideology of Social Reform*. This work explores how events and personalities have influenced the development of modern church teaching. By calling Catholic social thought an ideology, Camp means to reject the view that church teaching descends from the rarefied air of absolute principles. uncontaminated by the relativities of time and space. Rather, the teaching is a bricolage: an assortment of sources, methods and conclusions nudged forward as much by human history as by divine revelation. This does not, however, prejudice the integrity of the teaching. After noting the historical vagaries behind Leo XIII's *Rerum Novarum*, for example, Camp still thinks it 'one of the leading social documents of modern times'.[10] In Camp's view, one may criticize church teaching while respecting it as an ideology – meaning a body of associated ideas about society and human life based on a reflective quest for truth.

Juan Luis Segundo takes a different non-pejorative approach to the issue of ideology and Catholic social teaching. According to Segundo, church teaching is ideological in the sense that – like any social teaching – it represents a method of action. Ideologies, he says, are a 'systematization of objective knowledge about efficacy', or ways to get things done.[11] As such, ideologies are derivative; they apply a meaning-structure (or faith) to life, but are not the meaning-structure itself. While it is true that 'faith is never faith without ideologies and that an ideology without faith is never an ideology', the two must remain distinct.[12]

Though Segundo defines Catholic social teaching as an ideology, he thinks it a poor one. This is because the church creates and presents the teaching more as a faith than a method. The documents typically enjoin scripture, announce concepts, and 'work up a model of social study, of what ought to be' without 'simultaneously working out an effective methodology for implementing it'.[13] For this reason, Catholic social teaching seldom motivates people. This – and not Catholic sloth – explains why 'there is no society where . . . the social encyclicals have been put into practice in structural terms'.[14]

This analysis of representative commentators shows the main lines of how the ideological use of Catholic social teaching is understood today. From within the distinct insights and issues raised by these approaches, the question emerges: does any one of them help us understand 'official' Catholic social teaching as a whole?

The 'official' interpretation of ideology

Church authorities insist that Catholic social teaching is not an ideology. However, the meaning of this claim is blurred by the equivocal interpretation given to the concept 'ideology' in church documents. Sorting out this ambiguity helps to clarify the church's understanding of social teaching.

The words 'ideology' and 'ideological' appear often in post-conciliar social documents. They are commonly used in negative reference to 'liberal capitalism' and 'Marxist collectivism'. To these, the Latin American bishops add the 'doctrine of national security'.

While each of these ideologies is thought to suffer unique shortcomings, all share a common problem; they purport to give a 'final and sufficient explanation of everything' without positive reference to Christian faith.[15] The Popes and bishops find this problematic on two grounds. First, because the 'decisive criterion for truth can only be a criterion which itself is theological', it is 'only in the light of faith and what faith teaches us' that one most adequately understands humanity and society.[16] Second, because faith is fundamentally an existential event and not a theoretical proposition, it 'continually breaks down the horizons within which [human] understanding likes to find security' and thereby provides a power which urges people to 'go beyond every system and every ideology'.[17]

Ideologies are flawed, then, because their claims are incomplete and their horizons are fixed; the necessary tension between truth and openness is lost. It is on this basis (and combined with copious critiques of specific ideologies) that 'official' Catholic social teaching maintains a largely negative view of ideology.

Yet there are also church statements which put ideology in a positive light. In the Latin American bishops' Puebla document, ideologies are considered 'necessary for social activity, insofar as they are mediating factors leading to action'.[18] In this remark the bishops draw a distinction between two senses of ideology. One sense construes ideology negatively, as an incomplete and fixed theory about the overall nature of humanity and society. Another sense takes ideology to mean a concrete, local consensus of opinion which allows otherwise diverse people to solve their immediate social problems.[19] It is the latter sense which the bishops judge favourably.

This positive sense of ideology draws upon John XXIII's distinction in *Pacum in terris* 160 between 'false philosophical teachings' and social movements which may have 'originated from those teachings'. While the Pope forecloses Catholic acceptance of the former, he permits cautious participation in the latter. In the minds of the Latin American bishops, John XXIII's teaching means that Catholics cannot accept comprehensive ideological systems, but can participate in ideologies which express local aspirations for just social change.

Though room has been made in church teaching for a positive understanding of ideology (depending on its scope and function), none has been made for the idea that Catholic social thought is itself an ideology. In *Sollicitudo Rei Socialis* 41, John Paul II clearly rejects the idea that 'the Church's social doctrine' is 'an "ideology"'.

The logic of the 'official' position can be outlined as follows. Catholic social teaching is not a negative ideology because it is rooted in Christian faith. Faith expresses truths necessary for an adequate understanding of humanity and society and instils an exploratory dynamism in the heart of Catholic social teaching. These truths and this dynamism are neglected or denied in the negative ideologies of 'liberal capitalism', 'Marxist collectivism', and the 'national security state'. In *Sollicitudo Rei Socialis* 41, John Paul II assumes this perspective when he says that Catholic social teaching 'belongs to the field, not of "ideology", but of "theology"'.

Catholic social teaching is not a positive ideology either. It does not exist to provide specific answers to local problems. John Paul II's comment in the aforementioned encyclical is typical: 'The Church does not have "technical solutions"' and 'does not propose specific economic systems or programmes'.

Catholic social teaching is considered non-ideological by virtue of the middle position it occupies between negative and positive ideologies. In this way, too, the church joins a seemingly ambiguous assessment of ideology with an unambiguous insistence on the non-ideological status of its own social teaching.

The value of ideology to Catholic social teaching

Church authorities would insist that their teaching is distorted if it is treated as an ideology. However, if one adopts an inclusive definition of ideology and uses it to analyse church teaching, the result not only enriches our understanding of 'official' social thought, but reinforces a tensive balance central to the teaching itself.

In its recent *Guidelines for the Study and Teaching of the Church's Social Doctrine in the Formation of Priests*, the Congregation for Catholic Education makes two crucial observations about the deep structure of Catholic social thought. In section 7 the Congregation notes that church teaching can neither 'be neutral' nor be 'reduced to a biased philosophy'. Four sections later, it adds that social teaching must occupy a middle ground between 'the Gospel' and 'concrete reality'.[20]

The deep, tensive structure of Catholic social thought is reflected in this attempt to respect each point on the two axes of opposition: neutrality and bias, gospel proclamation and concrete application. At its best, church teaching finds itself at the intersection of these axes, midway between all four points. At its worst, it slides too far towards one point, producing teachings of vacuous neutrality, dogged bias, abstruse pronouncement or invasive application.

One way to identify and prevent such sliding is to analyse the literature in the light of all the ideological uses of Catholic social teaching discussed above. In other words, one should ask simultaneously: does this document mask social interests or conceal social strain, does it only advance social ideas or does it exclusively concern itself with generating social action? Each question warns against a particular imbalance.

By asking if a church document masks institutional interests, one remains alert to the possibility that a text may contain inappropriate bias. This works to preserve the balance of the literature in the direction of appropriate neutrality.

In monitoring the degree to which a church document may conceal social strain, one tests the likelihood that a given text may display a false neutrality or seek to avoid conflict. Being alert to these matters preserves the balance of the literature in the direction of acknowledging bias.

By checking a document's level of abstractness one monitors the degree to which a pastoral letter neglects its own practical application. Such checking preserves the balance of the literature in the direction of generating social action.

In noting if a church document is either invasive in its demands or overly ambitious in mobilizing the laity, one stays alert to the possibility that the letter is avoiding a discussion of its underlying ideas. Attention to this issue helps to preserve the balance of the literature in the direction of clarifying its ideas.

Treating Catholic social teaching as an ideology need not lead to distortion. Applying an inclusive understanding of ideology to the literature not only enriches one's understanding of Catholic social teaching, but reinforces the tensive structure of the teaching itself.

An investigation of the ideological uses of 'official' Catholic social teaching involves more than an inquiry into the power interests of the church. It involves a multiform analysis not only of the concept of 'ideology', but also of Catholic social teaching itself. Through this process, our understanding of both is enhanced.

Notes

1. Karl Marx and Frederick Engels, *The German Ideology* ed. C. J. Arthur, New York 1970, 64.
2. Talcott Parsons, *The Social System*, New York 1951, 356.
3. Clifford Geertz, *The Interpretation of Cultures*, New York 1973, 218.
4. *The German Ideology* (n.1), 123.
5. Renzo Bianchi, *Liberalism and Its Critics*, Northfield, Minnesota 1958, 56f.
6. Marie-Dominique Chenu, 'The Church's "Social Doctrine"', *Concilium* 140, 1980, 72, 74.
7. Chenu unfavourably notes the retun of the phrase 'social doctrine' in the speeches of John Paul II. See Marie-Dominique Chenu, *La 'doctrine sociale' de l'éqlise comme idéologique*, Paris 1979, 13.
8. Paul F. Lakeland, 'Ethics and Communicative Action: The Need for Critical Theory in Catholic Social Teaching', *Thought*, 1987, 61.
9. Ibid., 64, 67.
10. Richard L. Camp, *The Papal Ideology of Social Reform*, Leiden 1969, 12.
11. Juan Luis Segundo, *Faith and Ideologies*, Maryknoll 1982, 27.
12. Ibid., 142.
13. Ibid., 128.
14. Ibid., 127.
15. Paul VI, *Octogesima Adveniens*, 28, in Joseph Gremillion, *The Gospel of Peace and Justice*, Maryknoll 1976, 498.
16. Congregation for the Doctrine of Faith, 'Instruction on Certain Aspects of the "Theology of Liberation"', in *Origins*, 1984, 199.
17. *Octogesima adveniens*, 37, in *The Gospel of Peace and Justice* (n.15), 502.
18. John Eagleson and Philip Scharper (eds.), *Puebla and Beyond*, Maryknoll 1979, 198.
19. This point is indebted to the helpful insights of Ricardo Antoncich in his *Christians in the Face of Injustice: A Latin American Reading of Catholic Social Teaching*, Maryknoll 1987, 144–61.
20. Congregation for Catholic Education, 'Guidelines for the Study and Teaching of the Church's Social Doctrine in the Formation of Priests', in *Origins*, 1989, 173.

The Originality of Catholic Social Teaching

Gregory Baum

The originality of Catholic social teaching

In this article I wish to offer a reading of Catholic social teaching that is located in the wider public debate about political and social theory. In this context I interpret Catholic social teaching as a developing intellectual tradition, guided by its own proper inspiration, that is at present making interesting contributions to the public debate.[1] To do this I make a clear distinction between the early phase of this teaching, from Leo XIII to Vatican II, and the later phase, bolder and more incisive, beginning with Vatican II and from 1971 on, reflecting the influence of the liberationist perspective adopted by the Latin American Bishops Conference (1968) held at Medellin.[2] The moment of discontinuity between the two phases and the radical nature of the second phase has not, in my opinion, always been fully appreciated.[3]

When modern, liberal society emerged through the democratic and the industrial revolutions, the Catholic church rejected modernity and identified itself with the conservative sector of European society. At the end of the nineteenth century, Leo XIII laid the foundation for an official Catholic social teaching by bringing together the reformist ideas developed by socially concerned Catholics during that century. He relied on the critical dimension of classical conservatism. In the British political tradition this is called enlightened Toryism. Here society is seen as an organic community, a body politic, involving co-operation. Interdependence and hierarchy, that is in need of constant reform and revitalization through ethical conversion: that is, through the submission of all members of the community, leaders and people, owners and workers, to the norms of justice. Here government is seen as standing above the conflict of the economic classes, promoting the common good of society and protecting the weak against exploitation by the strong. Catholic social teaching defended private property against the tenets of socialism and supported the unionization of labour against the demands or liberal capitalism and the free market.

While this social teaching contained strong reformist impulses, its main emphasis was on the organic unity of society, cooperation, shared values and respect for authority. The struggle for justice had to take place within this context.

At the Second Vatican Council and more especially after the impact of the Medellin Conference, Catholic social teaching adopted, transformed and integrated a number of radical, modern ideas – I shall specify three of them further on. While these radical ideas were in a certain discontinuity with past teaching, they were understood not as breaking the tradition but as generating a dialectic within that tradition and thus creatively advancing it. Interpreting these radical ideas in continuity with Catholic social teaching lifted them out of the problematic intellectual framework in which they were first conceived, and protected them from their reductionist implications and problematic consequences. It is here that I locate the originality of contemporary Catholic social teaching.

It is my intention to confine myself to three radical ideas in recent papal teaching: the notion of democracy, the preferential option for the poor and the cultural meaning of labour.

A participatory society

In the nineteenth century the Popes strongly repudiated liberal society, and even after Leo XIII, the official social teaching remained silent on the topic of liberal democracy. Catholics were uncomfortable with the liberal theory which saw society as atomistic individuals joining in a social contract that would guarantee their safety, protect their property and maximize their freedom.

A different concept of democracy, in keeping with Catholic theological anthropology, emerges in the writings of John Paul II. This concept offers a theoretical basis for civil liberties while remaining faithful to the communitarian understanding of society entertained in the Catholic tradition. This concept of democracy, moreover, has radical implications because it applies, as we shall see, to all human organizations, not only to civil society. According to John Paul II, it is the high destiny of human beings to assume responsibility for their social existence. In the past, Catholic social teaching tended to distinguish in society between the *maiores* (élites and leaders) and the *minores* (the ordinary people) and assign responsibility for decision-making in society simply to the *maiores*. By contrast, John Paul II teaches that all people are meant to have a share in responsibility for the institution.

Laborem Exercens applies this principle to industrial workers. Their dignity, their high vocation, entitles workers to participate in decisions on the work process and the use of the objects they have produced. If workers are excluded from this co-responsibility, as they are in capitalist industries and as they were in Eastern European communist enterprises, then they, the workers, are humiliated.[4] They are deprived of what is due to them. They suffer injustice. Workers are then treated as 'objects' of production while they are meant to be 'subjects' of production.

Solicitudo Rei Socialis applies the same principle to the political order. Here, too, people are meant to be 'subjects', or responsible agents, of their collective existence. They are entitled to participate in the making of public policy. Even if a government adopts policies that favour the common good and enhance the well-being of the citizens, the government in question cannot be called just unless it offers the citizens a share in making these policies. Governments are held to respect what John Paul II calls the 'subjectivity' of the people. Whenever an élite, a single party or a special body, exercises unchallenged control of a society, the people are deprived of their subjectivity, experience frustration and become victims of injustice.[5]

According to liberal social theory, the democratic ideal was to maximize personal freedom in society, while the Catholic theory proposes a concept of democracy that aims at maximizing personal participation. We note that in liberal theory, the rights of individuals are given and protected by the state and so are rights enjoyed only by recognized citizens, while in the Catholic theory these rights are grounded in the dignity of persons and so are human rights to which all human beings are entitled. The liberal theory promotes individualism and tends to undermine all non-contractual solidarities in society, while the Catholic theory with its emphasis on participation creates social relations, enhances the sense of community and generates social solidarity.

We note, however, that the Catholic theory is a radical one, since it applies to all institutions, including industrial enterprises. An institution can claim to be just only if it allows its members to share in the decision-making process. We note in passing that until now John Paul II has not yet applied this social theory to the organization of the Catholic church, the one institution in which he wields power.

The preferential option for the poor

In the 1980s, papal teaching came to acknowledge the preferential option for the poor. This preferential option, derived from the religious experience of base communities in Latin America, has been defended and explored by liberation theology and has received the approval of the Medellin and Puebla conferences.[6] The option for the poor is a commitment containing two dimensions, one hermeneutical and the other practical. It is a commitment to look upon society from the perspective of the poor, the weak and the marginalized, and to give public support to the joint struggle aimed at their emancipation.

This liberationist perspective was upheld in parts of the declaration *Justitia in mundo* made by the 1971 World Synod of Bishops held in Rome.[7] It was further developed and applied to workers and wage-earners in John Paul II's *Laborem Exercens*. Here we were told that the dynamic element of industrial society, capitalist or communist, was the struggle of workers for the conditions of justice. Because labour produces the goods people need and, more importantly, creates people's consciousness and culture, labour can be said to generate society. It is for this reason, the encyclical argues, that the labour movement, conscious of its vocation and struggling for the rights due to workers, is the historical agent of social change in modern society.

In order to achieve social justice in the various parts of the world, in the various countries and the relationships between them, there is need for ever new movements of solidarity of the workers and with the workers. This solidarity must be present whenever it is called for by the social degrading of the subject of work, by exploitation of the workers and by growing areas of poverty and hunger.[8]

While the earlier Catholic social teaching looked upon society, including modern society, in an organic way, *Laborem Exercens* – in line with the preferential option – adopts a conflictive view of modern society, where certain sectors, the workers and the poor, are structurally exploited or marginalized, which is to say deprived of what is in justice due to them. Justice will come to society only as the deprived sectors become organized as a social movement and with the support of all citizens who love justice, struggle for the reconstruction of society.

In the same paragraph, *Laborem Exercens* hints that a similar principle is operative in the poor countries of the south. In their historical situation it is the poor and oppressed, that is the great majority, 'the people', who are called to be the agent of social change. Here, too, justice demands solidarity of the poor and with the poor. A few years later *Sollicitudo Rei*

Socialis regards as a positive sign in the contemporary world the growing awareness of the solidarity of the poor among themselves, their efforts to support one another, and their public demonstrations demanding greater justice. The church, we are told, 'is called to take its stand besides the poor, discern the justice of their requests, and help them satisfy them, without losing sight . . . of the common good'.[9]

The last words of the above quotation suggest the principal difference between the preferential option for the poor and the Marxist preferential option for the proletariat. The Catholic option divides society, and in the name of justice sets the workers (and in other contexts, the poor) against the powerful upholders of the oppressive and exploitative structures, but it does so not only for the sake of improving the material conditions of the disfranchised, but also and especially for the sake of the common good, for the ethical and spiritual well-being of the whole society. Space does not permit me to develop this argument. What is clear in the teaching of John Paul II is that 'sinful structures',[10] i.e. unjust social, economic or political mechanisms, not only produce suffering and misery among the victims, but also damage the humanity of the people who derive benefits from these structures and harm the common good of society by making it less democratic, or participatory, as defined above. Sinful structures weaken the spiritual substance of society as a whole. Since the liberation of the victims here serves the common good, the preferential option for the poor preserves the continuity with traditional Catholic social teaching.

This option for the poor also differs from the option for the proletariat because 'the poor' are not defined in purely economic terms. 'The poor' include the exploited workers and the people deprived of the material means of well-being, but they also include other marginalized groups: those who suffer from ethnic discrimination, the physically handicapped, the mentally retarded, and old people who have become helpless. An analysis of power and powerlessness also reveals that in all societies, though in different ways, women have been structured into positions of dependency and inferiority. Until now, we note, the Vatican has refused to recognize 'feminism' as a legitimate liberation movement struggling for fundamental justice.

Just as the Catholic concept of democracy borrowed elements from the liberal tradition and transformed them substantively into a social theory in continuity with the communitarian tradition supported by Catholic social teaching, so the preferential option for the poor has borrowed elements from the Marxist tradition and transformed them substantively into a social theory that recognizes the primacy of the common good as well as the non-economic aspects of poverty, and thus remains in continuity with Catholic social teaching.

This brief analysis suggests that it would be quite superficial to think of contemporary Catholic social teaching as a 'third way' between liberal capitalism and Marxism collectivism. Catholic social teaching does not look for some sort of middle ground between these two economic world-views. On the contrary, it regards both of these world-views as deficient, based in divergent ways on purely economic concepts of the human being. In my opinion, Catholic social teaching here makes an original contribution to social theory and the contemporary debate on the future of society.

Work as culture

Another substantive transformation of an idea taken from the Marxist tradition is the theory of labour developed in the encyclical *Laborem Exercens*. In this document, John Paul II defines human beings as workers, even while recognizing that they can also be defined by other essential characteristics.[11] Human beings must create the conditions of their survival and well-being by labour. Through labour they create their own world, and in doing so they unfold their powers and talents, realize themselves, and become what they are meant to be according to God's plan.[12]

Labour creates the world to which people belong and which in fact they constitute. In the sinful condition in which we find ourselves, labour is also the instrument that damages and distorts people's lives.[13] The organization of labour is the cause of personal alienation and social and economic inequalities. 'Work is a key, probably the essential key, to the whole social question'.[14]

Apart from the Marxist current of thought, few philosophers have recognized that human beings constitute themselves through work, that the values and ideas of people, including their very consciousness, are largely created by their labour. The word 'largely' is important here because other factors also affect the awareness of people. Because *Laborem Exercens* deals with the miseries, distortions and dehumanizing conditions of the present, it puts almost exclusive emphasis on labour.

Through labour people constitute their world, and in doing so they simultaneously realize themselves. What shape people's minds, therefore, are not the ideas proposed to them by teachers, preachers, or political leaders, but the conditions of their daily work. The organization of labour in industries, business, offices and other enterprises largely decides whether people on the whole will be co-operative or competitive, whether they will be intelligent, always developing their minds, or become unthinking and dull; whether they will be creative, open to new ideas, or become attached to a routine and afraid of experiments. Labour, in

Laborem Exercens, is a part of culture, in fact the principal part. We are made, or unmade, by the work we do.

John Paul II's theory of human beings as workers differs substantively from Marxist philosophy because the Pope fully preserves the primacy of the spiritual. Distinguishing between the 'objective' pole of the labour (the products made, the objects that surround us) and its 'subjective' pole (the self-realization of the workers through their work), *Laborem Exercens* assigns an unchallengeable 'pre-eminence' to the subjective pole.[15] In the evaluation of labour, of the industries and the entire labouring society, the primary importance is given to the effects of this labour on the workers. Does labour serve their subjectivity? Does it promote their freedom, their virtue, their creativity? While the product of labour is enormously important, priority is given to the spiritual.

If with John Paul II we adopt the anthropological definition of culture as the set of institutions, customs, values and ideas that define people's relation to one another and express the common ethos, then labour is part of culture, in fact the principal part. If a society is to become just, responsible and participatory, reconstruction must begin with the economic order, especially the organization of labour.

I note in passing that in the three radical principles mentioned above, the ethical dimension is preserved and at the same time perceived from a new perspective. Catholic social teaching, as I noted above, has always insisted that social reform demands a conversion of morals on all levels of society. This has often been interpreted as the proposal that if people only became more just, more generous and more selfless, the existing conflicts and problems of society would straighten themselves out. The call for moral conversion has been heard as an ideological strategy to defend the established order. Yet in the new perspective of contemporary Catholic social teaching, ethical *metanoia* is demanded to serve and strengthens the political struggle for the transformation of structures.

In this article I have tried to establish the originality of Catholic social teaching. Some of my Catholic colleagues do not accept my reading of the ecclesiastical documents because, they argue, these texts must be interpreted in the light of the actions and practical policies adopted by their authors. There are, however, 'special moments' in the life of religious and ethical organizations when the officers in charge are willing to bracket for a time their institutional interests and reflect on the meaning and power of the religious and ethical principles for which their organization stands. These 'special moments' may not occur very frequently, and the wisdom that emerges in them may not have much impact on the subsequent practical decisions made by the officers. Still, the wisdom formulated at these moments deserves to be heard and interpreted out of these texts themselves. If read in this way, I have argued, Catholic social teaching constitutes an original intellectual tradition that makes important contributions to the contemporary debate.

Notes

1. I have defended this reading of the evolution of Catholic social teaching in a book, *Theology and Society*, New York 1989. For a similar reading see also Donal Dorr, *Option for the Poor: A Hundred Years of Vatican Social Teaching*, Dublin 1983.

2. A similar reading of the evolving social teaching at the World Council of Churches would also reveal an initial inspiration and a bold, new thrust that make an original contribution to the secular political science debate of today.

3. The shift to the left in liberation theology and Catholic social teaching has been assessed by socialist economists and political scientists in North America. Socialist periodicals, such *Monthly Review* and *In These Times*, carried articles on the new Catholic teaching, and two socialist economists edited books dealing with this topic: William Tabb (ed.), *Churches in Struggle*, New York 1986; Michael Zweig (ed.), *Religion and Economic Justice*, Philadelphia 1991.

4. 'We can speak of socializing only when the subject character of society is ensured, that is to say, when on the basis of his work each person is fully entitled to consider himself as part owner of the great workbench at which he is working with everyone else', *Laborem Exercens*, 14.

5. *Sollicitudo Rei Socialis*, 15.

6. Cf. Dorr, *Option for the Poor* (n.1), 157–162, 207–17.

7. *Justitia in Mundo*, 3–6.

8. *Laborem Exercens*, 8.

9. *Sollicitudo Rei Socialis*, 39.

10. *Sollicitudo Rei Socialis*, 36–37.

11. 'Work is one of the characteristics that distinguish man from the rest of creatures, whose activity for sustaining their lives cannot be called work. Only man is capable of work, and only man works, at the same time by work occupying his existence on earth' (*Laborem Exercens*: introduction).

12. 'Work embraces all human beings, every generation, every phase of economic and cultural development, and at the same time it is a process that takes place within each human being, in each conscious human subject. Each and every individual is at the same time embraced by it. Each and every individual, to the proper extent and in an incalculable number of ways, takes part in the giant process whereby man "subdues the earth" through his work' (*Laborem Exercens*, 4).

13. 'Man's life is built up every day from work, from work it derives its special dignity, but at the same time work contains the unceasing measure of human toil and suffering and also the harm and injustice that penetrate deeply into social life within individual nations and on the international level' (*Laborem Exercens*, 1).

14. *Laborem Exercens*, 3.

15. *Laborem Exercens*, 6.

II · Reception of Catholic Social Teaching in Diverse Lands and Groups

Catholic Social Teaching in Germany between Competing Trends

Stephan H. Pfürtner

Ubi amor, ibi Deus – *for Paulus Engelhardt, unfailing in his friendship, on his seventieth birthday*

1. There were – and are conflicts

'Encouraged and fortified by *Rerum Novarum*, during the Kaiser's empire the German Catholics had played a leading part in constructing and developing social policy. Unfortunately a passionate dispute flared up among them over the nature of the association so warmly commended by the Pope . . . The view of the integralists was that for Catholics there should be only a workers' association led by a priest, which would have to take on all responsibilities; the great majority of the workers wanted their own trade union organization led by the workers themselves.' These are the opening words of Oswald von Nell-Breuning's chapter on the 'German Trade Union Dispute' at the turn of the century in *Texte zur katholischen Soziallehre*.[1] He mentions the 'passionate dispute' among 'the German Catholics at the time of the Kaiser's empire', with 'integralists' on one side and the 'great majority of workers' on the other.

The topic in dispute is evident: the relationship between the German Catholics and the rising trade unions. This was no genteel dispute. 'The Berlin branch of the Federation of Catholic Workers' Unions fought against and vilified the great majority of the other branches in the Federation from West, South and East Germany, which were well disposed towards the trade unions' is the way in which Nell-Breuning describes the situation.[2] The conflict even extended to the Fulda bishops' conference, and some of the bishops appealed to Pius X in Rome. 'Against the hardest resistance of the integralists, who had considerable influence on him (viz., the Pope), they succeeded in wresting a concession from him. In very limited circumstances and on very strict conditions, they (viz., the bishops) could "tolerate" the membership of Catholic workers in interconfessional trade unions.'[3]

So in this historical process there were two issues in dispute:

1. Should the church grant the Catholic workers a degree of self-determination in their own concerns and release them from their close ties to the hierarchy with the aid of the clerical president?

2. Should an alliance be allowed between the Catholic workers and their Protestant colleagues with a view to forming Christian trade unions?

In the confessionalist polemics of the time the majority of bishops and clergy saw the latter course as a kind of betrayal of the 'true church'. By contrast, the Catholic workers wanted to strengthen their Christian understanding of life and politics by the alliance, and along with their other Christian colleagues also to serve what in their eyes was the better cause of the workers' movement. The integralist church circles evidently failed for decades to perceive this loyalty of the Catholic workers and their trade union leaders to their convictions about the faith.

Rather, they nurtured a deep-seated mentality of mistrust in Catholic circles of anything with the name 'trade union'. Similarly, the Christian workers of the time were branded traitors to the workers' movement by the members of the 'free' trade unions with their militant atheistic tendencies. For with their ties to 'the rich church' and to religion – in Karl Marx's well-known phrase the 'opium of the people' – in the eyes of the 'Marxists' they were surrendering the workers' cause to the class enemy. In this situation, in which their identity was under severe threat, the Catholic workers were largely abandoned by their church. Only a few clergy and theologians took their side. Nell-Breuning very soon became one of them and began a passionate fight for the just cause of the worker's movement. Today he is a 'solitary witness of the century' to it.

'The trade union dispute' is something like a historical case study with a significance which extends far beyond the attitude of German Catholicism to the 'social question' of the nineteenth and twentieth centuries. First of all, it demonstrates that even in the Roman Catholic church of the time, which often seemed so monolithic, the situation was by no means 'harmonious'. This situation and its consequences are still relevant today. There was no practice of public dispute in the church, any more than there is one now. 'Faithful dissent', to use Charles Curran's phrase,[4] is still anathematized, and minorities which have often demonstrated their loyalty to faith and church are dismissed out of hand as 'deviant'. Secondly, there was a debate over the coming of age of the laity and with this over a new collaboration in the church. Laity no longer wanted to be regarded as recipients of instructions from the hierarchy or as its extended missionary arm, but as partners who were competent to judge and to act. It is illuminating that it was not least the workers' movement which prompted this process of 'democratization' within the church. In the same way, the 1906 electoral victory of the Liberals, with the help of those workers who had the vote, contributed to the breakthrough to modern democracy in Great Britain. This process proved to be of decisive significance for the European democratic movement.[5] Thirdly and finally, we need to note the ecumunical dynamic in the trade union dispute. The dispute broke out at a time when public language did not even have the word 'ecumenism' to use, and in many countries a 'mixed marriage' still entailed the excommunication of the Catholic partner.

The dispute presents challenges to the church which in the view of wide circles in German-speaking Catholicism have yet to be solved. The 'Joint Synod of the Dioceses of the Federal Republic of Germany' which met in Würzburg in 1975 resolved to recognize the laity as members of the church in their own right, above all in questions where they were professionally competent, and indeed to accord them a place in the proclamation of the word and preaching in the liturgy.[6] What has been the practical result of this? Still under the inspiration of the Second Vatican Council, *A Memorandum of German Catholics. Edited by the Bensberg Group*, produced in 1970, called for the 'democratization of the church' – with an explicit justification for the use of this term.[7] The regression of the Vatican authorities in this connection in the episcopal nominations in Cologne, Chur and Vienna sparked off a church conflict in German-speaking Catholicism which was as extensive as it was intense. And what about the relationship of the church to the cause of the workers' movement? It is still relevant that the joint synod in Würzburg mentioned above entitled its 'Resolution on the Church and the Workers' 'an ongoing scandal'. 'This lamentable fact,' the resolution continues, 'finds eloquent expression in the world-famous remark of Pius XI to Cardijn, his lament that the great scandal of the nineteenth century was that the church had lost the workers. Our country, too, is no exception to that, despite the great achievements of social Catholicism.'[8] The text of the synod offers material enough to indicate that the scandal continues, and how it does so.

2. Some 'oral history' – a complex of problems as a stimulus to thought – the method of presentation

The development of Catholic social teaching in Germany or even in the German-speaking world cannot be described in any degree of detail here, but it would be a rewarding theme for an extensive research project. At the same time it would be an interesting piece of the history of political Catholicism in Germany over the last 150 years – and not of course unconnected to German social and political history generally. It would tie in well with existing works.

It is also impossible to give a detailed bibliography here. Anyone looking for accounts of, or introductions to, Catholic social teaching in Germany might refer to Oswald Nell-Breuning's *The Social Teaching of the Church*, with his comments on the magisterial teachings of the Popes and the last council;[9] to the *Introduction to Catholic Social Teaching* which I edited with Werner Heierle;[10] or to the two discussions of political history by Franz Klüber: *Catholic Social Teaching and Democratic Socialism* and *The Revolution in Catholic Social Teaching*.[11] Another recent work is the brief systematic survey by Lothar Roos.[12]

Here I simply want to draw attention to some competing expositions of papal social teaching in German Catholicism and to some topics of conflict, above all since 1945. I feel it appropriate also to add some 'oral history' from my own experiences during this period. This may perhaps be more illuminating than a systematic discussion of the theoretical points in dispute. Moreover, without such reminiscences some things worth thinking about will be lost for ever.

German Catholicism had its own situation of conflict. For France, 'the Lefebvre affair' in recent decades recalled the struggle there between political and ecclesiastical integralism and any democratic, social and ecumenical openness.[13] For Spain it is enough here to refer to the way in which numerous church circles were involved with the Franco régime. It is evident that the key content of the German trade union dispute was bound up with far-reaching processes of social and political history in Europe. It was a signal for the historical rise of German political Catholicism in opposition to a confessionalistic, closed church which had become questionable because of the interests it shared with the middle class, dominated by capital and with nationalistic leanings.

What was involved here was not only 'the social question' but also the preparations for a new international Europe; here too there was also a new linkage within the church – for example between the Catholic workers and the clerical hierarchy – and a new relationship between the church and secularized society and between the church and the other confessions. Was there to be church integralism or an open church in an open society? This was the basic theme of the wide-ranging discussion. Relevant movements in France, for example those connected with the 'worker priests', were followed with interest in the open circles of German Catholics.[14] But as in France, so too in Germany papal social teaching had no politically effective support. As I have already pointed out, the Catholic workers' movement was only a minority in the church, and moreover was still often viewed with mistrust in the Catholic sphere. So magisterial social theory was outlined 'from above', by the Popes and their collaborators (the identity of whom was kept strictly secret), and not developed and supported by a broad church movement 'from below'.

The questionable consequences of this lack of support, which I have warned about elsewhere,[15] can hardly be taken seriously enough. Marie-Dominique Chenu has stressed one of the negative effects. What happened was that the theological 'context' of Catholic social teaching was not the oppressed workers themselves but those who were reflecting on them. Thus not only did the teaching come into being from the perspective of a centuries-old tradition of church supervision and patriarchy, but it also risked being understood as a kind of philosophy of the essence of human community, as an ideological system of abstract, unhistorical principles, which had not come into being out of the situation of human beings in their real need, and therefore did not remain committed to this need.[16]

Some neo-conservative Catholic social ethicists with a good deal of political influence in the Federal Republic (and beyond) have constantly attempted to interpret Catholic social teaching in this way and make it fundamentally opposed to liberation theology. Here one might mention not least the hermeneutical position of H. J. Wallraff, according to whom Catholic social teaching represents 'a structure of open statements'.[17] 'Open statements' logically call for an open church – open in its language and its teaching, and open not least to the workers' movement, with its call for welfare for the industrial proletariat and democratic involvement in politics. Historically this development in the church first made itself felt only tendentially; it came to be expressed more clearly in the Weimar Republic (1919–1933) and was brutally ended by the Hitler regime. As is well known, the National Socialist terror swept away the Christian trade unions along with the others. After the war there was a new beginning. And this is where my personal account begins.

3. Walberberg: a case study – In memory of Eberhard Welty

The German Dominican house of studies in Walberberg, near Bonn, to which I belonged, soon became a centre for socially and politically committed Catholicism in post-war Germany. The impetus for this came from Laurentius Siemer, at that time Provincial of the German Dominicans, and Eberhard Welty, for a long time Rector of the Hochschule. Through their dedication, a group of younger members of the order, most of them returning home after the war, contributed to the development. Siemer had been so intensively involved in the resistance, having numerous contacts with the key figures in the 20 July 1944 plot, that he would have shared the latters' fate at a popular tribunal had he not gone underground at the last moment to escape the Gestapo, and 'disappeared' for the rest of the war.

Many members of, or sympathizers with, the resistance groups of the time had one experience in common: in trenches or sick beds, in prisons or concentration camps, they had experienced a new human bond which went through all confessions and parties, through all social classes and social strata, through all European nations and cultures. In the oppression caused by the inhuman régime of Hitler and his henchmen they experienced a new solidarity. The urgency of the cooperation of all 'men of good will' had been made clear to them by the extent of the injustice, cynicism and destruction. The social and political activities of Laurentius Siemer had begun in Walberberg and Cologne as early as 1941, initially in close contact with leading men in the Catholic workers' movement. Jakob Kaiser, Johannes Albers, Karl Arnold, Bernhard Letterhaus and Nicolaus Gross were among them, and also further forces, above all from the Centre Party. Carl Goerdeler was sometimes a guest, as was Alfred Delp. After the end of the 'Third Reich', on 17 June 1945 there was a conference in Cologne of members of the former political underground from the Rhineland who had survived the War and the Nazi terror. There was a parallel initiative under Jacob Kaiser in Berlin, separated by the occupation zones. Those involved committed themselves to political reconstruction in Germany. Welty was a member of the Rhineland group. It stood for a social and political consolidation of all Christian forces and thus for collaboration with interested German Protestants. The former confessional integralism of the Centre Party had disintegrated, and the basic conception of the Christian Democrat union had been born. But it was not just a matter of building interconfessional bridges.

Eberhard Welty, who came from a working-class family, was particularly interested in ending the old hostilities between the most politically active of the workers and the Catholic church in Germany, and looking for new ways to collaborate in building a new and socially more just future for Germany. Soon after the war he made contact with leading representatives of the Social Democrats and the trade unions. (I still remember the handwritten letter of condolence which Herbert Wehner wrote to the

Dominican convent at Walberberg after Welty's death because of his close personal association.) With Hans Böckler, the chairman of the German Trade Union Federation from 1949, and his group of colleagues, there were various conversations and attempts at collaboration.

Welty exerted a decisive influence on the founding of the Christian Democratic Union.[18] He had been able to rescue the minutes of the sessions of the Cologne-Walberberg circle since 1941 from the hands of the Gestapo. Using them as a basis, at the very first conference of this group after the end of the war on 17 June 1945 he was able to present the document *What Now? Principles and Suggestions for the New Order in Germany*.[19] Leo Schwering, an important member of the group and the conference, and a historian of 'the first hour' and the first phase of the CDU, did not just see the document as 'the testament of witnesses who had shed blood' but also described it as a programmatic expression of the social and political ethos at which this founding group of the CDU aimed in their further meetings and drafts.[20] As early as 1946 Welty was able to follow it up with an extensive development of the programmatic sketch under the title *Decision for the Future*. The subtitle, a repetition of the *What Now?* of the earlier document, indicated the continuity.[21]

In retrospect the introduction, written at the Walberberg convent, which at that time was still being used as a wartime hospital, reads like a historical document. 'Today is 7 March of the year 1945, the last year of the war. The evening before last, on 5 March 1945, our house here was occupied by troops of the American army, just as our community had gathered in the shelter for supper . . . Exactly a year ago, on 6 March 1944, the author was able to present a first, shorter section of this work for examination and approval. Then came 20 July 1944, with the manhunt which followed. Unfortunately, more than one of the group which asked for this paper has fallen victim to the executioner. Our people needed these high-minded men so much . . . True, the group from which the instigation came is a small one . . . But all were and are caught up in the holy, earnest will to serve the German people with utmost honour and loyalty, averse to any local narrowness. It is particularly significant that the group includes not only men of learning and business, but above all leading men from the former Workers' Movement (disbanded in 1933) – they form the majority.[22]

Anyone looking for historical threads in terms of substance or persons leading to the drafting of the Basic Law of the Federal Republic of Germany should not ignore Welty's work. After the collapse of the 'German Reich' the churches were the only major organizations still functioning. Those political forces which had not been compromised sought the help of the churches in the process of reconstruction. Welty was one of those who devoted himself with the utmost concentration to this political and theological *diakonia*. After a basic introduction, on the Christian order of life orientated on God's will, he prefaced all further remarks with a confession of human dignity. 'Human dignity is unassailable,' runs the well-known Article 1.1 of the Basic Law.[23] The preamble puts 'responsibility before God and man' at the head of the whole Basic Law. In Welty's document, a new definition of the relationship between natural law (willed by God) and positive law (enacted by human beings) and of church/Christianity and state was followed by an appreciation of the family, the right to life, the right to personal and public freedom, the right to property and to education. As a whole the work stands in the context of grappling with the destruction of life and law by National Socialism. Throughout, it presents the vision of a new order. One might compare the first nineteen articles of the Basic Law with it. *Decision for the Future* can be termed a preliminary draft for the study that the Walberberg social ethicists produced for a wider public between 1951 and 1958 in three volumes, in *Herders Sozialkatechismus*.[24] The work was widely influential, in Germany and abroad, and was even translated into Japanese.

4. A test case: property law

I have selected one theme from a wealth of programmatic themes. In the chapter on property law, Welty wanted on the one hand to endorse the right to private property, but on the other hand to put unmistakable stress on the obligations to society or the community which this right entailed:[25] 'A new order must come, and the law for its inner formation certainly and finally excludes the division of society into the haves and the have-nots, and the other abuses associated with that. The whole distribution of commodities and property must come about quite differently from before. It will not come about of its own accord; it must be introduced by legal and constitutional measures.'[26] The author takes his basic guidelines not only from papal social teaching but also from Thomistic social theology and philosophy – supported by the contemporary Thomas-renaissance. According to Thomas this earth is given to all human beings. All should draw sustenance for life from it. In the sight of the Creator God, all human beings should have a right to use its goods for the basic needs of life. Welty (basing himself on A. Horvath) stressed that the real natural law lay here. So 'private property' was not a 'strict law of nature'. 'The order or distribution of property which has come into being through history goes back to a human institution.'[27]

In so doing he also aimed at releasing the Catholic church from its one-sided entanglements with the property-owning middle class. Historically, such ties had not grown up as strongly in German Catholicism as in German Protestantism. In the period of the Kaisers and the Weimar Republic, political Catholicism had been almost completely concentrated in the Centre Party, which to some degree also reached out into the working class. But the working class did not in any way have an influential representation in it. Moreover, the 'Centre' was sharply distinguished from the international socialism of the time by its confessional tie. Conversely, its leading representatives saw the condemnation of socialism by Leo XIII above all as an alliance between the church and the rich. They saw the papal repudiation of contemporary socialist plans for expropriation simply as the endorsement of the existing situation over property in favour of the ruling class.

Nell-Breuning investigated this assumption in an illuminating discussion. In it he went into the denunciation of the common interests of 'the church and the rich' and at the same time was able to demonstrate the fundamentally false interpretation of *Rerum Novarum* (1891). By a slack translation or 'even by a deliberate falsification', the official German version of the encyclical had made the Pope say that he 'canonized' the existing situation over property.[28] But the Latin wording and context of *Rerum Novarum* leaves no doubt that while on the one hand Leo XIII defended the fundamental right of human beings to private property, on the other hand he explicitly charged the state 'to regulate the use of property in keeping with the requirements of the common good' (RN 35). Certainly it was almost another century before Paul VI finally and clearly overcame the sacral tabu on the existing property situation. He even agreed to the expropriation of ancestral property by force – albeit only in the extreme instance 'where there is manifest, long-standing tyranny which would do great damage to fundamental personal rights and dangerous harm to the common good of the country' (*Populorum Progressio*, 1967, no.31). But Nell-Breuning rightly pointed out that Leo XIII was already arguing for an equitable change to the pattern of property-holding:[29] 'So the "acquisition of resources by the workers" can already be found in *Rerum Novarum* (RN 35)'. Nell-Breuning remarked that it was a 'nonsensical, indeed monstrous assertion that Leo "canonized" property'[30] and had rejected state intervention over possessions in order to regulate the use of property better. 'In reality, Leo says that God left it to human intelligence and initiative to shape the order of property (RN 7). It is hard to understand how such false translations and interpretations could be accepted for decades without any church office finding occasion to take steps about them.'[31] I would add that this is hard to understand, given the real task of the church. However, things become quite clear if we regard the misleading terminology as a sign of the main interests which have shaped German Catholicism from the time of the Kaisers to the present.

5. Joint bridge-builders with a similar fate in the church: Welty and Nell-Breuning

After the war, the closeness of their basic orientation in social and political ethics soon brought Eberhard Welty and Oswald von Nell-Breuning together at different levels. On the Catholic side, during the 1950s, for all the differences in their methodological approach, these two men were part of the small group of committed theologians who succeeded in building a bridge with German Social Democracy. That came about not least through their collaboration in the de-ideologizing of the Social Democratic party programme in the 1959 'Godesberg Programme', as a result of which the old Marxist hostility to religion was abandoned. It also came about through their crucial demonstration from the Catholic side that it was wrong to suppose that in the social encyclicals the Popes had condemned socialism outright: this condemnation applied only to a particular form of socialism.[32] As a result it now became possible even for convinced Christians to involve themselves politically in Social Democracy.

What both sides had in common was an acknowledgment of the dignity, the inter-personal solidarity and the social obligations of human beings. As early as 1945, Kurt Schuhmacher (a leading figure in the reorganization of the Social Democrats and the leader of the party from 1949) had already repudiated the total socialization of human beings. He declared that Social Democracy was based 'on respect for the human personality'.[33] The Godesberg programme developed this line in many ways. It acknowledged that socialism strove for a society 'in which the individual can develop his personality in freedom, and as a serving member of society can share responsibility in the political, economic and cultural life of humanity'.[34] Since Leo XIII the Popes had adopted precisely this social and political middle way. For they were equally opposed to the old liberal lack of concern among the economically successful for society and the socially weaker, and to any kind of social totalitarianism which defined the person merely in terms of utility for a particular collective and those holding power in it.[35] Welty and Nell-Breuning together insisted on collaboration between Catholic social teaching and this form of socialism.

'Father Nell' – as he was known to his intimates – had meanwhile achieved considerable public recognition in Germany and abroad.[36] He was regarded as the 'grand old man of Catholic social teaching'. He played a crucial part in the preparation of the encyclical *Quadragesimo Anno* (1931). He succeeded in inspiring scholars both inside and outside the Jesuit order, and also politicians and journalists. Nevertheless he did not win any great sympathizers or even friends among the official representatives of German Catholicism. In an appreciation on his eighty-fifth birthday, evidently on the basis of direct information from Nell-Breuning himself, Roman Leick remarked: 'No bishop ever thought fit to visit Nell-Breuning in his sparsely-furnished room, though the German episcopal conference comes often enough to the Philosophisch-Theologische Hochschule St Georgen in Frankfurt, where he has held the chair of Christian Social Teaching and Ethics since 1928. It causes Nell-Breuning considerable pain that sometimes years go by during which he cannot exchange a single word with a bishop, far less be asked for his professional advice.'[37] In 1980, when questioned on television as a 'witness of the century', Nell-Breuning himself commented: 'I could imagine that some pressure was put on my superiors that I should give up my connections with the Social Democrats and the trade unions. But my superiors stopped that.'[38]

The works of Eberhard Welty have almost been forgotten, not least because of his comparatively early death (on 2 June 1965, at the age of sixty-three). His fate in the church was similar to that of Nell-Breuning, but with one difference. Welty had many conversations with Cardinal Frings, then Archbishop of Cologne – indeed even a friendly relationship with him. My researches indicate that Frings insisted that the first printing of the programmatic work *What Now?* should be withdrawn and 'toned down'. Nevertheless the Cardinal shared Welty's basic views, and after the war invited him to his house for a regular round of discussions on social and political questions. These meetings took place between representatives of employees and employers; in them Welty primarily represented the interests of the employees. Furthermore, as early as the end of 1946 the Dominicans had created *Die Neue Ordnung* (The New Order), a bi-monthly journal for questions 'in church, state, society and culture', as the sub-title went. He looked after the periodical for almost twenty years as its chief editor, and developed it into a discussion forum for a wide circle of authors outside and inside the church. In the middle of the 1950s, not least on his initiative, a number of training courses for trade unionists were held in Walberberg, each lasting for several weeks. I took part in a number of them.

I still have a vivid memory of the sense of discovery on the part of those involved in breaking down the hostile images cherished by both the old 'long-serving' shop stewards and us with our ideas about 'trade unionists' or 'Sozis', shaped by the Catholic milieu. Through our conversations, to our surprise we became aware of a basic shared attitude and a new sense of solidarity. It is not as if all the divides between us were filled in. But in the constructive discussion with the other 'class representatives' we developed and put into practice a model of our own interests. Something of this kind was to come about later in the discussions between employers and employees in Germany over free collective bargaining. Class struggle on the old model aimed at the elimination or at least the crippling of the opposing class. After the war, the trade unions in other European countries with their communist orientation had this as their aim, and the Thatcherism which arose from the capitalism dominant in Great Britain rediscovered the aim for itself. But how successful did this prove for the national economies of the countries concerned with the new impoverishment of the 'have-nots'?

Pius XI had called this 'old model' of social controversy a 'poisoned' or 'reprehensible class struggle'.[39] But this was not a general condemnation of the militant advocacy of class interest. Rather, he insisted that the bitter conflict could 'change into honourable controversy between the classes carried on out of a concern for justice. It certainly does not represent the social peace which is longed for on all sides, but it can and should serve as a starting point from which to work towards a harmonious collaboration between the classes.'[40] Welty quoted the papal text in his 'social catechism', and stressed its significant elements.[41] In the Walberberg training weeks with the trade unions, he and his collaborators put particular stress precisely on this historically new outline. The learning process which began here may, among other things, have encouraged some young Dominicans to follow the example of the French worker priests in their own way, in the Ruhr.

Welty's practical concerns and principles did not go unscathed. Although, as I have said, he is to be recognized as one of the founder members of the Christian Democratic Union,[42] and even after that kept up many connections with Christian Democrat leaders in work and dialogue, he was soon labelled 'Red Welty' in politically conservative Catholic circles. The CDU had vigorously dissociated itself from its own social and economic conceptions as sketched out in the Ahlen programme of 1947. The leading light behind this tendency – and thus also the main opponent of the broad outlines of a 'Christian Socialism' along the lines of the Ahlen programme – was Konrad Adenauer. He had not taken part in the discussions of the founding group of the CDU in the Rhineland, but came from outside. His influence probably resulted in the farewell to a dream of a new, socially more just, world of the kind that the Cologne-Walberberg group had striven for, supported above all by Christian trade unionists and businessmen under the theological inspiration of Siemer and Welty.[43] It was a thorn in the flesh to Conservative pragmatists of political Catholicism that the Catholics were no longer – as in the past – clearly committed to one party 'in the name of the church'. In practice, that of course meant that above all the Social Democrat door was opened to the Catholics. I cannot say whether this tactical partisan view had persuaded Konrad Adenauer to move against Eberhard Welty, or whether there were yet other reasons. Be this as it may, along with a chosen few initiates among the leadership of the Dominican order in Germany at that time, in the middle of the 1950s I discovered that Adenauer had pressed the Superior General in Rome to remove Welty from Walberberg. The General rejected this suggestion.

However Welty, who was anything but a tough old campaigner, was wounded by being attacked in this way. Moreover the religious and political forces of integralism began increasingly to gain the upper hand within the German order. In addition, Heinrich Basilius Streithofen, whom Welty had himself once included among his young collaborators, had stabbed him in the back. Unexpectedly, Streithofen had come out publicly against the united trade union and had argued for the splitting-off of the Christian trade unionists. Sweeping in his analyses and intemperate in his language even then, to all intents and purposes he already advocated at that time what he later argued for in the North Rhine-Westphalia Landtag elections of 1985: 'The social committees (viz. of the CDU) have suffered a severe blow in their very homeland, namely in the industrial centres of the Rhine and the Ruhr. They have no say in the German Trade Union Federation. The Federation, for long an organization with a socialist bias, is misusing them, simply as an extended arm among the Christian Democrats. The chairmen of most industrial trade unions seem to be socialist politicians.'[44]

For Welty, any rabble-rousing was an abomination. He was well aware of the difficult situation of Christians in the German trade-union movement or in particular trade unions. However, in his eyes the common cause of the workers called for strong trade unions. So in a committed way he tried to oppose any splitting of them, especially polemical splitting of the Catholic workers unions. He therefore argued for the strengthening of 'Christian-social comradeship in the German Trade Union Federation'. One need only read the informed and fair discussion of this question in his works[45] and compare it with the language of Streithofen, to recognize that the present 'Walberberg Institute for Social Science' in Bonn has only the name in common with the institute founded by Welty.

6. Are past histories only of regional interest or experiences of international significance?

The 'case studies' reported above bring into focus far more than local disputes on a minor level. Basically they need to be consulted and interpreted against the horizon of the future of our world. Certainly it seems that as a result of the betrayal by Stalinism of the basic ideas of socialism, and the economic and political disaster in the countries where formerly 'socialism really existed', everything has been decided in favour of a bourgeois conservative exegesis of Catholic social teaching along the lines of Adenauer and the Christian Democrats and their approach to social policy. However, this appearance may prove fundamentally deceptive. Nothing is yet decided on a worldwide basis. The social tensions between the industrial proletariat and the property-owning middle class in the previous century have long been continuing on a new and much more radical level. The divide between the people in prosperous societies and those dominated by world famine is gaping ever wider. At the same time the number of those within the prosperous societies who are falling into the poverty trap is increasing to a terrifying degree. If that is the case – and, given the facts, who could doubt it? – then the verdict of history is still open as to whether the way taken in Germany by bourgeois conservative Catholicism has not fundamentally undermined the social and political ethos of Catholic social teaching.

More than developments in Germany are at issue here. For the forces of political Catholicism which I have mentioned have had influence through a variety of channels in church and society on many countries of the 'Third World', especially in Latin America. I have already referred to the actions taken against 'liberation theology' in which, on the initiative of Bishop Hengsbach of Essen and von Streithofen, the 'Study Group on Church and Liberation' has been involved in since 1973.[46] However, we still lack any comprehensive research here. Such research will have to uncover the share in responsibility for the rise of mind-sets which in the meantime have led to radical conservatism over property with its consequences of closer involvement with the military dictatorships and even the terror of the death squads and other marauding bands in these countries. It is well known that the massacre of the Jesuits in San Salvador is only the tip of the iceberg.

The admonition of a 1961 Walberberg working party involved in the preparations for the Second Vatican Council on the central guidelines of Catholic social teaching has lost none of its topicality (Eberhard Welty was primarily responsible for the section quoted):[47]

1. 'The supreme principle of the primary natural law (is) that the goods

of the earth are there for all, and therefore that the whole order of property remains unconditionally subject to "general use", to the "common use of all" (Thomas Aquinas II–II 66.2), the "original benefit of all" (Pius XII). This principle in no way applies merely to interpersonal encounter or simply within a national economy; it also applies to the world economy, and to all orders of property and distribution among the nations.' This critical principle is used to analyse particular situations and the following conclusion is drawn:

2. 'The *latifundia* situation which is still dominant in many places, i.e. an extremely unjust distribution of land, and the intolerable material, moral and social wretchedness which goes with it, along with the unavoidable duty of land reform or the giving away of land' remain prime themes of social policy in numerous countries. 'The church itself should everywhere make available for social purposes any possessions in property and land which it does not urgently need to fulfil its own specific purposes . . .'

3. The concentration of economic power has to be opposed all over the world. 'There should be an adamant warning against the injustice, the dangers and the damage which can or must arise for society, the economy, the state or the family of nations . . . (as a result of this). These economic concentrations of power must wherever possible be avoided and where necessary reduced to a proper level. Here it makes no difference who are behind the concentration, whether they are parties, interested groups, big business, monopolies, or states and blocks of states.' There is an admonition to pursue 'possibilities of rational "disentanglement" and appropriate foundations for laws and forms of harmonious co-operation on a national and international level'. Finally,

4. The basic outlines of economic demcracy are drawn and stressed. In the steps of Pius XII, 'responsible circles' are called on 'to improve traditional criteria of distribution and to involve the employees more in the life, the responsibility and where appropriate in the product of the enterprise'.

It is now thirty years ago since these four basic guidelines were written. It could be extremely illuminating today to reflect on them against the background of widespread social and political tension, not least in the Latin American countries which derive from a Catholic tradition, with their anti-democratic forces and their extreme violations of human rights, but also in connection with the tremendous concentration of power by big business with its preponderance towards the political community in the United States, in Germany or the European Community. The political and economic collapse of the countries of the former Eastern block is a no less interesting illustration of the four basic guidelines. Certainly a new threat to humankind has arisen through the ecological crisis of this planet. But that in no way deprives the basic postulates I have quoted of their substance. On the contrary, the ethos of social and political justice expressed here takes on a new quality, and its urgency is even further intensified.

Translated by John Bowden

Notes

1. Oswald von Nell-Breuning, Introduction to *Texte der katholischen Soziallehre. Die sozialen Rundschreiben der Päpste und andere kirchliche Dokumente*, ed. by the Bundesverband der Katholischen Arbeitnehmer-Bewegung Deutschlands, Kevelaer [3]1976, 13f.
2. Ibid., 14.
3. Ibid.
4. Charles E. Curran, *Faithful Dissent*, Kansas City 1986.
5. Richard Thoma, *Wesen und Erscheinungsformen der modernen Demokratie: Grundprobleme der Demokratie* (1949), ed. Ulrich Metz, Wege der Forschung CXLI, Darmstadt 1973, 66–106: 77.
6. *Gemeinsame Synode der Bistümer in der Bundersrepublik Deutschland. Beschlüsse der Vollversammlung. Offizielle Gesamtausgabe* I, edited for the Praesidium of the Synod . . ., Freiburg, Basle and Vienna 1976, 169–85, 609–14.
7. *Demokratisierung der Kirche in der Bundesrepublik. Ein Memorandum deutscher Katholiken, Herausgegeben vom Bensberger Kreis*, Mainz 1973.
8. *Gemeinsame Synode* (n.6), 327.
9. Oswald von Nell-Breuning, *Soziallehre der Kirche. Erlaüterungen der lehramtlichen Dokumente*, Vienna 1977.
10. Stephen H. Pfürtner and Werner Heierle, *Einführung in die katholische Soziallehre*, Darmstadt 1980 (with bibliography).
11. Franz Klüber, *Katholische Soziallehre und demokratischer Sozialismus*, Bonn and Bad Godesberg 1974; id., *Der Umbruch des Denkens in der katholischen Soziallehre*, Cologne 1982.
12. Lothar Roos, 'Soziallehre, katholische', *Evangelisches Staatslexikon*, Stuttgart [3]1987, Vol.2, cols.3231–40.
13. Yves Congar, *Der Fall Lefebvre. Schisma in der Kirche?*, Freiburg, Basle and Vienna 1977; Ludwig Kaufmann, 'Econe unter Lefebvre – eine Sekte?', *Orientierung* 39, 1975, 118–20; id., 'Im Schatten der Konterrevolution. Geschichte und biographische Notizen zum Traditionalismus von Erzbischof Lefebvre', *Orientierung* 41, 1977, 156–60.
14. Paulus Engelhardt, 'Priester in "dieser" Welt', *Die Neue Ordnung* 9, 1955, 14–22, 74–83.
15. Pfürtner and Heierle, *Einführung* (n.10), 44–6.

16. Marie-Dominique Chenu, *La doctrine de l'église comme idéologie*, Paris 1979: cf. also *Concilium* 1980.

17. H. J. Wallraff, 'Die katholische Soziallehre – Ein Gefüge von offenen Sätzen', in *Normen der Gesellschaft (Nell-Breuning Festschrift)*, ed. H. Achinger et al., 1965, 17–48.,

18. Rudolf Uertz, *Christentum und Sozialismus in der frühen CDU. Grundlagen und Wirkungen der christlich-sozialen Ideen in der Union 1945–1949*, Stuttgart 1981, 23ff., 112ff. The work is a thorough study with information and comment on the theme in this period.

19. Printed as a manuscript without place or date; reprinted in facsimile in a special number of *Die Neue Ordnung*, September 1985.

20. Uertz, *Christentum* (n.18), 30.

21. Eberhard Welty, *Die Entscheidung in die Zukunft. Grundsätze und Hinweise zur Neuordnung im deutschen Lebensraum*, Heidelberg 1946 (for the 'British Zone', Cologne 1946).

22. Ibid., 7f.

23. *Grundgesetz mit Deutschlandvertrag, Menschenrechts-Konvention, Bundeswahlgesetz, Bundesverfassungsgerichtsgesetz und Parteiengesetz*, with an introduction by Günter Düring, Munich [16]1975.

24. Eberhard Welty, *Herders Sozialkatechismus*, 1. *Grundfragen und Grundkräfte des sozialen Lebens*, Freiburg im Breisgau 1951–58; id., Vol.2, *Der Aufbau der Gemeinschaftsordnung*, Freiburg im Breisgau 1957; id., *Die Ordnung des Wirtschaftslebens. Arbeit und Eigentum*, Freiburg im Breisgau 1958.

25. Welty, *Entscheidung* (n.21), 331–51.

26. Ibid., 333f.

27. Ibid., 335.

28. Nell-Breuning, *Soziallehre* (n.9), 43; cf. id., *Texte* (n.1), 69f.

29. Nell-Breuning, *Soziallehre* (n.9), 43.

30. Ibid.

31. Ibid.

32. Klüber, *Soziallehre* (n.11), 30ff.

33. Quoted ibid., 31.

34. *Godesberger Programm*, no.7, quoted in ibid.

35. Pfürtner and Heierle, *Einführung* (n.10), 5ff.

36. Wolfgang Schroeder, *Orientierung* 54.3, 1990, 25–9; Alfred Horne, *Publik-Forum*, 23 February 1990, 14f.; Helmut Schmidt, *Rheinischer Merkur*, 7 March 1980; Ulf Fink, *Die Zeit*, 9 March 1990; *Frankfurter Rundschau*, 7 March 1990.

37. Romain Leick, 'Der Papst berief den unbequemen Mahner. Die Kirche verdrängt ihre eigene Soziallehre', *Vorwärts* 6, March 1975, 7.

38. Noted by me from the repeat broadcast on Zweites deutsches Fernsehen on 6 March 1970 at 23.40, on the occasion of the centenary of Nell-Breuning's birth.

39. Pius XI, encyclical *Quadragesimo Anno* (1931), 114.

40. Ibid., cf. Nell-Breuning, *Soziallehre* (n.9), 59ff.

41. Welty, *Sozialkatechismus* 1 (n.24), 315f.

42. Uertz, *Christentum* (n.18), 23ff., 112ff.

43. Ibid., 72–111.

44. Heinrich B. Streithofen, 'Das Vertrauen zurückgewinnen. Die Konditionskrise der CDU von NRW verlangt eine Neubesinnung', *Die Neue Ordnung*, special issue, September 1985, 14.

45. Welty, *Sozialkatechismus* 1 (n.24), 229ff.
46. Pfürtner and Heierle, *Einführung* (n.10), 59ff.
47. 'Walberberger Dominikaner zur Umfrage in einer Gemeinschaftsarbeit', in *Was erwarten Sie vom Konzil?*, special issue of *Wort und Wahrheit* 10, 1961, 688–97.

The Reception of the Social *Magisterium* in Italy: Themes and Discussions

Alberto Melloni

The state of the church and politics in Italy on the eve of the promulgation of *Rerum Novarum* was backward compared with that of the other countries of Europe: its industrial development was still modest and geographically circumscribed; the episcopate for the most part came from the lesser nobility; and the theologians and educated laity showed little capacity for analysing the social situation of the country. What in historical perspective appear to be the forerunners of the Catholic social action which came into being in connection with the encyclical were creative and scattered voices: the 1891 encyclical was to give them vigour and impulse, offering above a unitary framework for the initiative and the opposition to it scattered through the church's structure.

Among these initial factors are some which were to be the main features of the Italian reception of *Rerum Novarum*, whether in the shorter or the longer term: (i) the fact that the nature of social teaching[1] was defined from within the specific Italian context; (ii) the difficult relationship between the Italian episcopate and the Pope, who was not a born primate; (iii) the burden placed on the ecclesial development of the country in the crucial decades when the Roman question was the focal point in church and politics and tended to imprison the papacy in the role of political opponent of the unitary state and authentic protagonist and validator of the relationship between Christianity and society; (iv) the tendency of the political forces of Italian Catholicism to exploit this peculiarity in the position of the Pope and to rely on his authority, slowing down the growth of the church's awareness.

In themselves, these are factors which do not relate exclusively to the development of social teaching and the century of its history. That needs to be said, because there could and should be a good deal of discussion in depth as to whether and how far Leo XIII's encyclical is really a prominent enough milestone in terms of content to put out of mind the former interventions by the Pope, who as a temporal sovereign was himself part of the dynamics of European politics, in what were described by Ballerini in *Civiltà Cattolica*, 20 January 1877, 264, as 'all political matters relating to faith and custom', appealing in the process – in various forms – to that 'myth of Christianity' which ultramontane thought put forward and accepted.[2] At all events, it is on these features of the relationship between church and society that I would like to dwell in the brief space available to me, in an attempt to bring together the phenomena and key terms (some of which I shall emphasize) with which the social teaching was received in Italy. We must keep at least three levels directly in mind: the development of direct social action, which suffered a serious crisis with the endorsement of Fascism and the Lateran Treaty; the political presence, which social action fostered and absorbed; and the weak material ecclesiology which characterized the Italian church and affected the dynamics of the reception.

Historically, the interaction between these levels created a circularity between the Catholic movement,[3] the subject and object of the reception, the Italian church, and the pontiffs, who were called upon to demonstrate the theological and political utility of social doctrine and to make it an instrument which would bring together the episcopate and the laity (including, and often primarily, the Italian episcopate and laity).

I

It will be evident that, right from the beginning, *Rerum Novarum* in fact owed a good part of its success in Italy to the fact that as an act of the pontiff it had an effect on the episcopate and mobilized over the issue of working conditions a church which was still wavering between a transference to industrial society of the ideology of the poor and the paternalistic and corporative theories of the kind put forward by Taparelli d'Azeglio in *Civiltà Cattolica*. The commitment of pioneers like Toniolo (theoretician of a Christian democracy and in 1889 promoter of the Catholic Union for Social Studies) or Fr Liberatore (author in 1889 of a study on the workers' associations) could in fact have pointed the way: however, they were not in a position to put the network of relationships in Catholic Italy at the service of the impulse towards solidarity (born out of a rivalry with the socialists which was not always barren). Deprived of a complete identification with the church and seeking to be in harmony with the Pope's statements (which were issued in increasing numbers after Vatican I and given wide publicity by the press), the parishes and dioceses were opened up to initiatives which were important for the workers and the national economy.

The mutual aid societies among the workers are evidence of this: in Italy these came into being less in the human débris of industrialization and more in the areas where there was active religion, even running counter to economic development (here the Piedmont of Cardinal Gastaldi was an exception). The importance of the fabric of relationships of trust which was created around the clergy can be confirmed at various levels: one might think of the series of Casse rurali which played a role in agricultural conditions; or the Unioni rurali which, thanks to their relationship with those institutions which had a broadly-based shareholding, could spring up throughout northern Italy: from 1894 they even had a journal providing information and instruction, *La cooperazione popolare*. Other ventures in the agricultural economy include the experiments with practices like collective leases, an invention of the socialists of Emilia which was soon adopted in areas with large estates, for example by Monsignor Portalupi in Lombardy and Don Sturzo in Sicily.

2

The ferment which Leo XIII also created in this sector was not caused so much by the explosiveness of his positions as by the fact that they legitimated what broad strata of the church viewed with mistrust:[4] they did not so much bring to birth as create a haven for hopes which otherwise would have been in danger.[5] That would emerge with the return of mistrust which characterized the pontificate of Pius X: the initiatives were not radically different, but the changed climate tended to emphasize in many of these initiatives that social modernism which gave substance to the fears of employers close to the dioceses and opened the way to the progressive affirmation of a policy of social action.

Under the pontificate of Pope Leo XIII and at the beginnning of that of Pius X the *non expedit*[6] had allowed the development of original and sometimes highly abstract political schemes, but these were also more suspect and were put down harshly. There are, for example, the cases of the difficulties over the development of trade unionism, for which Medolago Albani sought the support of the Pope to counter the suspicion of the bishops; of Catholic feminism;[7] of democratic Catholicism with the various ways in which it was understood (up to the encyclical *Graves de Communi* with which Leo XIII intervened);[8] and of Murri's idea of the political contribution of 'Christian principles' to interpreting the democratic law.[9] These are fragments of a dynamic reception of the papal *magisterium*, which was first to be disowned by theological charges of social and political modernism (the encyclical *Pascendi* of 1907) and then defeated in the framework of an ideological mobilization of the church which took a heavy toll of its exponents, along with the modernists, through informers and the repressive judgment which was so much part of the living forces of Catholicism.

On the social, theological and political level the result was a progressive rhetoric of moderatism. In the first place there was a return of the Pope's rhetoric of freedom, demanded in the face of the authority of the unitary state: the constant dramatization of the end of temporal power was a political and ecclesiastical banner around which Italian Catholicism could be mobilized, first of all through abstentions and then in more active forms, but always maintaining the perspective of seeking to make Italy and its church a safe haven for the papacy, its needs and its directives.[10] There was also a return of the rhetoric about the mandate entrusted to the laity by the hierarchy in temporal matters, which appeared in *Il fermo proposito* (1905), promulgated the year after the difficulties with the *Opera dei congressi* and the Catholic committees.[11] Moderatism was also to become evident in the form taken by the various unions: by the choice of the Secretariat of State, the diocesan presidencies were to go to men with episcopal and papal backing in the country, thus intervening to guarantee the pledges of *Edita Saepe* (25 February 1910); and then the Gentiloni pact of 1913 which brought Giolitti the Catholic vote. There was also a return of anti-capitalist rhetoric, as a result of which the failure to recognize economic liberalism no longer generated new initiatives but provided a counterpoint – albeit rhetorical! – to active and militant anti-socialism.

There are traces of this moderatism in the Settimane Sociali, convened for the first time at Pistoia in 1907 by the Unione Popolare: a bishop often spoke at them, but only to repeat the *magisterium*, and in so doing would give a moral analysis priority over one of economic issues. Interrupted by the outbreak of war and resumed from 1920 to 1934, from 1945 to 1970, and again this year, for sixty years the weeks have remained an important point of reference for a Catholicism like that of Italy, which at the beginning of the century even more than now appeared culturally incapable of using synodical instruments.

3

The great crisis of the War, the perception of the power of socialism and the end of the pontificate of Pius X created a different situation: the ecclesiological failing of the Italian church continued, but original research began again. In 1914, in the wake of Murri, Guido Miglioli inspired the birth of the Sindacato Nazionale dei Lavoratori Cristiani; the same leader also guided the agricultural trade union of Cremona towards an agreement which related to an 'interest in the profits and not to a share in the products'. This important idea, accepted at the famous Lodo Bianchi on 8 June 1921, was revoked on the introduction of the Fascist agricultural pacts, but it is evidence of a new stage in initiatives. It was Benedict XV who in this area too recovered something of Leo's openness: the favourable climate revitalized the growth of the white economy (co-operation and trade unionism) in competition with the socialists and communists, allowed the birth of the Partito Popolare in 1919, and gave legitimacy to Sturzo's efforts to confront the economic needs of the country as such.[12] Arguments like those set out by white trade unionism in the Settimana Sociale of 1912 for the economic support of the strikers (put into practice by Monsignor Radini Tedeschi, the bishop of Bergamo, whose secretary was the future John XXIII) could be discussed again, strengthened by the successful establishment of the mass Catholic organizations;[13] there were also important successes in the financial world. In 1914 the Federation of Catholic Banks came into being and finally systematized the Institutes (the Banco Ambrosiano, the Piccolo Credito Bergamasco, the Banco di Roma and the Casse rurali). which up to that point had been operating separately. Through the foundation of the Banca del lavoro e della cooperazione, it tried to plough back into the countryside the surplus of deposits from the rural banks.

4

The post-war period and Fascism led to a conflict between social action, the church as it was, and ecclesiastical aspirations: it was not difficult to persuade towards moderatism a Catholic hierarchy which saw Rome and Italy as a kind of papal enclave, something quasi-sacred.[14] That caused a crisis not only for the roots of popularism but also for Catholic trade unions, welfare (the Opera Bonomelli collapsed in 1928) and economics,[15] suffocated by the peace agreement arrived at between the Holy See and the state through a concordat between the Vatican and the Fascist regime. This happened at the very point when the move away from Fascism was developing and there was budding anti-Fascism among Italian Christians. This was caused by the highly rarefied impulses of the hierarchy[16], in the context of which the quest for political control of the Catholic consensus imprisoned the Italian church and its primate.

Quadragesimo Anno (1931) reflects these contradictions: whereas the stress on the anniversary pointed back to Leo's model, the context stressed its rhetorical profile. In fact Pius XI took up the thesis of the subordination of economics to ethics as part of a defence of the utility of social doctrine: this further widened the gap between the abstract distancing from liberal postulates (similar to the Fascist criticism) and an effective condemnation of the principles of Leninism and socialism. Here was an implicit toleration of the theory about Christianizing Fascism which circulated to such a degree in Catholic circles in Milan and Rome. For a whole generation of Catholic Italians (those who would become part of the resistance in the north of the country), the 1929 treaty and concordat and *Quadragesimo Anno* were the last piece of a past to which they did not belong. Moreover, at a more general level, the affirmation of Nazism, the choice of a collision course with Bolshevism and the approach of war[17] contributed to an acceleration of the crisis for the social *magisterium* which led to the solemn condemnations in 1937 (*Divini Redemptoris* on communism, *Mit Brennender Sorge* on Nazism, *Firmissiman Constantiam* on Mexico), all of them still not free of the myth of a Christian Italy.

5

The election of Pacelli and the outbreak of armed conflict marked the opening of a new phase. Pius XII, who did not issue any social encyclicals in the technical sense, was clearly aware of the crisis: having got through the war with the habit of silence,[18] he found the complex working-out of the great radio messages – a stimulus and very important support for some Italian political circles[19] – an instrument for guiding the growing Christian Democrat movement with skill and sensitivity.[20] In Italy the party was now a delta into which social action and economic enterprise, rural radicalism and social sensibility flowed: it was for the party to represent these interests and to bring together the consensus mediated by them.

However, that is not the end of the story. The acceptance of the form of democracy and then of a republic, the awareness of the challenge of reconstruction, the late impact of Maritainism, and the rivalry between the prelates of the Secretariat of State (Tardini and Montini), gave new impetus and protection to new classes of leaders, militants and faithful.[21]

The Catholic intellectuals finally embarked upon analyses of the economy and future projections: for example, at the end of July 1943 some Catholic economists (Paronetto, Saraceno and Vanone) had put in the *Codice de Camaldoli* the first new and not abstract plans for an economic programme; and in the 'Commission of 75' (1946) which was working on the Italian constitution, A. Fanfani interpreted instances of personalism in property law, while G. Dossetti and G. La Pira developed theories of social control over property and through the review *Cronache Sociali* introduced Keynesian elements. Be that as it may, the character of social teaching as a political discipline prevailed over its newer aspects.[22] In 1950, to pick a significant turning point, La Pira published two famous articles in *Cronache Sociali* on 'The Expectations of Poor People', in which he criticized a mechanistic conception of the economy and scientifically nourished ancient Catholic mistrust, rescuing it from the rhetorical impotence in which it had been imprisoned. In the same year, which also saw the birth of the Catholic trade union CISL, under Christian Democrat control, and the third anniversary of the final break-up of the unity of Italian trade unionism, Archbishop Siri of Genoa gave the inaugural lecture at the Settimani Sociali on the trade union question, stressing above all the duty of the workers' organizations to oppose communist and socialist organizations.

The regulation of this kind of dynamic, the effort to lead it back to the mandate and therefore bring it under the control – in theory – of the Pope,[23] came about by using the fabric and the institutions of the church itself: one example here is the condemnation of the collaboration of Catholics with communists.[24] Achieved at a point when the political experience of the Christian left was now exhausted,[25] it affected the Christian community as such, to the advantage of the political unity of the Catholics. This politicological myth (which came into being as a counter to secularization and the drop in the number of practising Catholics) gave an ideological authority to anti-communism, which was already in the majority in the social bloc of Italy and De Gasperi's Christian Democrats.[26]

A *magisterium* which sought to be open to universal horizons and principles, and said as much, restricted itself to political action with some ecclesiological corollaries: the persistent blurring of the role of the Italian church; the modest role which the Pope assigned himself; the compromise with the means of ideological propaganda through the civic committees; and the impoverishment of the church organizations (above all Catholic Action) by drawing off people and intellectual resources in a way that decapitated the local churches.[27]

6

The model for the reception of social teaching, by which what was in fact received and developed was not a *magisterium* but an ecclesiology in the making, broke up between 1958 and 1959. This was not the result of a change in doctrine or of the thrust of political radicalization but of the ecclesiology which John XXIII brought with him. Don Milani is quite clear that Pope John was trying to 're-establish the power of the bishops . . . John XXIII, first of all, gave autonomy to the bishops.'[28] In doing this John XXIII laid the foundations for the breaking of a bond which had now become oppressive for the Italian church. The convening of a council then produced a context in which Italian Catholicism would have to cope not with the brutal concretizations of power based on subtle political abstractions, but with the greatest and most fundamental questions of the life of the church in history.[29] John's attention to the church is in itself revolutionary. Pius XII had abandoned the genre of the social encyclical, but had interpreted its spirit; Pope John resumed the genre and concluded it with *Mater et Magistra*, produced in 1961 with the collaboration of the secretary of the Settimane Sociali, Pietro Pavan. It put an ideal seal on the seventy-year parable of the social *magisterium*. By this date political Catholicism had now come to include social Catholicism, the survival of which in the credit and cooperative system had electoral significance. The proposals for economic reform presented by the Dossetti group were now closed and the encyclical came – belatedly, in relation to such readings – to the problems of the economic imbalance in the world. These delayed intuitions now found an echo in the speeches made by Saraceno and Andreatta at the Christian Democrat meetings in San Pellegrino on 'Italian Society' (1961, 1962) and the report of Guido Moro to the Eighth Christian Democrat conference in Naples (1962).

7

It is widely recognized that *Mater et Magistra* is linked with the document which in the eyes of the Pope was to open a new era, *Pacem in Terris*. Already before the Cuban crisis and the opening of the council, in April 1963, Pope John, again making use of Pavan, declared the doctrine of just war closed and spelt out the consequences of the opportunity that the church had created by convening the council in the autumn of the previous year. The consequences of the superseding of the doctrine of the just war reached to the very foundations of social teaching, its original relationship with the ideology of the Christian society in which the church functioned as a supreme arbitrator. Here was an invitation to open a stage in which the gospel was proclaimed more strongly.[30] In reality, the subsequent course followed by Italian Catholicism – even leaving aside the failure to take up *Pacem in Terris* in the conciliar constitution *Gaudium et Spes* – did not embrace all John's intuitions – nor did it pay the price for all of them.[31] Nevertheless, those seeds – the experience of the council, the developments in ecclesiology, the reflection on the church of the poor – brought out the contradiction between the dynamic of communion and the political dynamic, in which for example Don Milani was involved. It proved possible for Paul VI's attempts to modernize the style of the reception of social doctrine to hide that – so that the Italian episcopal conference was limited to acting as the voice of its most authoritative member – but not to undo it.

8

That is not surprising. Paul VI belonged heart and soul to the period and the generation of the social *magisterium*. He made various attempts to depart from the pattern of the commemorative encyclicals, with *Populorum Progressio* and the institution of the Day of Peace. The fact that such attempts were both anticipated and developed at the international level (Medellín) or at the local level did not comfort the Pope: as happens more generally in conciliar reception, Paul VI often considered as prejudicial to his role and the unity of the church positions which, while not contradicting his *magisterium*, did not endorse it.[32] And so it was that in a climate of growing opposition, Paul VI reopened the cycle of anniversary encyclicals with *Octogesima Adveniens* of 1971. We are in the last seven years of the pontificate,[33] when even in Italy the Pope had to measure up to the contradictory crises in the growth of Catholicism, with the evidence of its quantitative diminution and its fall to become a minority, with increasingly widespread refusal to show obedience and communion in the ideology of political unity, along with the first assertions of the experience of movements to the detriment of episcopal authority – and sometimes authoritarianism.[34] Parallel to these difficulties for the pontificate, the Italian church had a hard task to qualify as a social force outside political references and in a strictly ecclesial sense;[35] here one need only cite the differences which arose over the conference on 'Evangelization and Human Promotion', the disastrous result of the referendum on the abolition of legislation on divorce (and then of that against on abortion), and the conflicts arising from the appearance of Catholics on the Communist Party list – from 1976 onwards.[36]

It is evident that the turning point was the election of the Archbishop of Cracow to the papacy. For Italy, however, a symbol of the end of an era had already taken place in the spring of that same year, 1978, when the Red Brigades – among whose militants were some who came from Catholic circles – kidnapped and then killed the Christian Democrat president, Aldo Moro, despite the ambiguous and impotent efforts of the state and the pontificate. In one of the extreme tests of Italian democracy, the pontificate did not succeed in taking up a position which was not a reflection and a part of the internal political game, with its darkest shadows. This was the collapse of a position which had claimed increasing areas of power, organized the consensus which legitimated it, constructed the ethical motivations which were to justify it – and then, when it came to the point, discovered that it was prisoner of the logic which it had thought to dominate.

9

By a historical coincidence, now in the 1980s,[37] this exhaustion was accompanied by the shock of the pontificate of Karol Wojtyla, which is the most radically new and characteristic fact of the last ten years and the immediate future. For the first time, Italian Catholics contended with a social *magisterium* which hardly, if at all, knew the vocabulary, the sensitivity, the links. Moreover, this came about in a political phase which, particularly in its last years, had to rediscover its own associations beyond anti-communism.

So the attitude of Christians fluctuated between an ostentatious reception, which sought to absolutize the Polish model in a version opposed to the state, and a politically more developed, mannered reception which now had its own originality and qualifications, but which worried about electoral competition enough to aim at presenting itself as the arm of the Pope against the 'neo-Protestants', whether these were bishops or laity.[38] In the course of the 1980s there was a lack of capacity to distinguish between these positions and go beyond them, and to give believers a degree of autonomy in the life of society which would free the church from its increasingly embarrassing forms of representation, whether by the Catholic Democrats or by the popular Catholics.

Nevertheless, this gave rise to interesting ferment almost all over the country, towards which neither discernment nor episcopal fatherliness were shown with any generosity.[39] There were clear signs of ambivalence and indeed ambiguity;[40] one might think, for example, of the remarkable mobilization of energy in the social services – the so-called voluntary sphere – in which both a radical charity and the recapture of social space in the crisis of the public services were expressed in the same sociological terminology. Or there was the choice by the Italian episcopate in the early 1980s to begin again from the bottom, practised with great commitment by diocesan organs and church movements, but not endorsed and defended by exploiting them to the point of making them part of Catholic identity. One might also consider the denunciation of the Mafia by the bishops and the conference with which they sought to make up for a long period of political silence, though risking a further and definitive break with that world of poverty which is more a victim than an author of the process of degeneration. Or, to take a last example, there is the question debated in various dioceses (Milan, Bologna and Turin) of the relationship between ethics and economics in which – as at the beginning of the developments which I have summarized here – the doctrinal aspect of the problem was filtered off from the dangers associated with the need for the Italian church to redefine its social role (perhaps including that of producing ethics) in the industrial context.

The original tradition of the social *magisterium* as a fact which ignores the life of the Italian church – when it does not prejudice it – sometimes seems to be returning. This is a symptom and a factor of the crisis in discernment and the new difficulties introduced by the personality of John Paul II. It can be seen in the numerous political schools which have emerged in the last five years as an expression sometimes of the bishop, sometimes of the ACLI, sometimes of the Society of Jesus, sometimes of Comunione e Liberazione, and recently, finally, of the Socialist party. The attempt to teach social doctrine and redirect Christians towards politics as such, the multiplicity of the experiments and the hostility that can be found between them show how a past stage is leaving its traces in the present.[41]

Translated by Mortimer Bear

Notes

1. Cf. M.-D. Chenu, *La doctrine sociale de l'Eglise comme idéologie*, Paris 1979.

2. Cf. D. Menozzi, 'Intorno alle origini del mito della cristianità', *Cristianesimo nella storia* 5, 1984, 363–400; G. Miccoli, *Fra mito della cristianità e secolarizzazione. Studi sul rapporto chiesa-società nell'età contemporanea*, Casale Monferrato 1985.

3. Cf. *Dizionario Storico del movimento cattolico in Italia 1860–1980*, ed. F. Traniello and G. Campanini (3 vols), Turin and Casale Monferrato 1981–1984, or *Storia del movimento cattolico in Italia*, ed. F. Malgeri (6 vols.), Milan 1980–1981, and the criticisms by G. Battelli, 'Ricerca storica e categorie mentali in recenti opere sul "movimento cattolico" in Italia', *Cristianesimo nella storia* 8, 1987, 227–44.

4. *Aspetti della cultura cattolica nell'età di Leone XIII*, ed. G. Rossini, Rome 1961.

5. For example, the petition on working conditions from the trade union congress was taken up and developed to apply to emigrants by bishops like Guidelli in Modena, Guidani in Bergamo, and Scalabrini in Piacenza.

6. Cf. M. F. Mellano, *Cattolici e voto politico in Italia. Il 'non expedit' all'inizio del pontificato di Leone XIII*, Casale Monferrato 1982.

7. Cf. P. Gaiotti de Biase, *Le origini del movimento cattolico femminile*, Brescia 1963, and more recently S. Zampa, 'A. G. Roncalli ed A. Coari: una amicizia spirituale', in *Giovanni XXIII transizione del papato e della chiesa*, ed. G. Alberigo, Rome 1988, 30–50.

8. For interpretation of the 'actio benefica in populorum', cf. *Romolo Murri nella storia politica e religiosa del suo tempo*, Rome 1972.

9. Cf. M. Guasco, *Politica e religione nel Novecento italiano. Momenti e Figure*, Turin 1988; C. Giovannini, *Politica e religione nel pensiero della Lega democratica*, Rome 1968.

10. Cf. F. Traniello, *Città dell'uomo. Cattolici, Partito e Stato nella storia d'Italia*, Bologna 1990, 8, for the appeal to these shared inspirations against a certain 'rigidity in the historical field of certain interpretative categories'.

11. Later on the stress would no longer be on the sender but on the content, i.e. the animation, but this did not change the perspectives.

12. For the particular situation in Lombardy see G. Vecchio, *I cattolici milanesi e la politica. L'esperienza del Partito Popolare, 1919–1926*, Milan 1982.

13. At the end of 1910, half of the Catholic trade union organizations were concentrated between Lombardy and Venice (more than 57,000 members); 40% of the industrial workers in trade unions (around 11% of the labour force immediately before the war) belonged to these associations.

14. For the nature of Rome as a symbol of the country cf. A. Riccardi, *Roma 'città sacra'? Dalla Conciliazione all'operazione Sturzo*, Milan 1979.

15. Between 1922 and 1925 the crisis hit the Banca del lavoro e della cooperazione (and ruined the Casse Brianzole), the Tridentine institutes associated with the Banca Cattolica di Trento, then the Credito Toscano, the Società Marchigiana Bancaria, the Credito Meridionale campano, the Credito Pugliese, etc.

16. For the episcopate and Fascism see G. Battelli, 'Santa Sede e Vescovi nello Stato unitario. Dal secondo Octtocento ai primi anni della Repubblica', in *Storia d'Italia (Einaudi). Annali 9, La chiesa e il potere politico*, Turin 1986, 837–46, and the bibliography; D. Veneruso, *Il seme della pace. La cultura cattolica ed il nazionalimperialismo fra le due Guerre*, Roma 1987, has different concerns.

17. F. Traniello, 'Il mondo cattolico e la seconda guerra mondiale', in *Città dell'uomo* (n.10), 169–228.

18. For the opportunity missed by the Holy See in the first half of 1939 cf. G. Dossetti, in his introduction to L. Gherardi, *Le querce di Monte Sole*, Bologna 1986, vii–lxvii; for the questions tied up with the attitude of Pius XII cf. the report by G. Miccoli, 'Aspetti e problemi del pontificato di Pio XII', *Cristianesimo nella storia* 9, 1988, 343–427.

19. Cf. P. Pombeni, *Il gruppo dossettiano e la fondazione della Democrazia Cristiana (1938–1948)*, Bologna 1979, and on the immediate post-war developments M. Casella, *Cattolici e Costituente. Orientamenti e iniziative del cattolicesimo organizzato (1945–1947)*, Naples 1987.

20. Cf. D. Menozzi, 'The Case of Italy', in *The Church and Christian Democracy, Concilium* 193, 1987, 62–71.

21. F. Traniello, 'La Chiesa e la Repubblica', in *Città dell'uomo* (n.10), 229–79.

22. For a new myth see P. Chenaux, *Une Europe Vaticane? Entre le Plan Marshall et les Traités de Rome*, Brussels 1990.

23. Cf. A. Riccardi, *Il potere del papa*, Rome and Bari 1988; id., *Il 'partito romano' nel secondo dopo-guerra (1945–1954)*, Brescia 1983.

24. G. Alberigo, 'La condanna della collaborazione dei cattolici con i partiti comunisti', *Concilium* 11, 1975, 1209–22.

25. *La Sinistra cristiana (1937–45)*, Brescia 1982.

26. Cf. G. Tassani, *La terza generazione. Da Dossetti a De Gasperi, tra Stato e rivoluzione*, Rome 1988.

27. Cf. A. Riccardi, 'The Vatican of Pius XII and the Catholic Party', *Concilium* 193, 1987, 62–71.

28. Cf. G. Alberigo, 'Santa Sede e vescovi nello stato unitario (1945–1978)', in *Storia d'Italia* (n. 14), 857.

29. Cf. my 'Formazione e sviluppo della cultura di Roncalli', in *Papa Giovanni*, Bari 1987, 3–54.

30. John XXIII himself had already provided a practical example in refusing to act as a beachhead to the Italian industrial world which was seeking allies against the nationalization of the electricity industry, cf. G. Miccoli, 'Sul ruolo di Roncalli nella chiesa italiana', in *Papa Giovanni* (n.29), 202f.

31. We need a documented study on the establishment of collaboration in the government between Socialists and Christian Democrats from John XXIII to Paul VI, which came about as a result of their refusal to support the plans of Fanfani and Moro.

32. The case of the removal of the Archbishop of Bologna, ordered the day after his firm condemnation of the American bombing of North Vietnam. See the 'Memoria' by G. Dossetti in *Chiese italiane e concilio* and the bibliography there.

33. *Paul VI et la modernité dans l'église*, École Française de Roma 1984.

34. For Comunione e Liberazione see *Gli estremisti di centro*, ed. S. Bianchi and A. Turchini, Rimini and Florence 1975; more recently F. Ottaviano, *Gli estremisti bianchi*, Rome 1986; from within the movement, M. Vitali and A. Pisoni, *Comunione e Liberazione*, Milan 1988.

35. It is symbolic that the Settimane sociali in 1970 exhausted themselves over this; see the collections, *Le Settimane sociali, 90 anni di storia dei cattolici italiani*, Roma 1989; *Il cammino della settimana sociale*, Rome 1989.

36. The communications of the Italian episcopal conference on the electoral question are worth studying; they are now in *Enchiridion CEI* (3 vols.), Bologna 1985–1986.

37. Cf. *Religione e politica negli anni '80*, ed G. Ruggieri, Casale Monferrato 1982.

38. The two positions have a noun in common: the one does not in fact fail to stress the inadequacy of faith if this does not produce culture; the other defends its autonomy in continuity with the political culture of democratic Catholics.

39. Note in this connection that the Italian church has been summoned to a convention (the last in Loreto in 1985), but never to a synod or a national council, which is the proper instrument of collegial government.

40. Events at the beginning of 1991, with the outbreak of the war in Iraq, could prompt similar reflections on the aspirations for peace expressed in various ecclesiasical contexts, but I will not draw conclusions from them here.

41. So what remains typical of the 'Italian case' and its course is the fact that the tensions within the church assume the character of historical polemic, as for example in the hurtful press campaign against Giuseppe Lazzati, who was accused of 'neo-Protestantism' because of a non-integralist conception of civil life, cf. D. Menozzi, 'Il sinodo sui laici ed i "novi movimenti": il "caso Lazzati"', *Cristianesimo nella storia* 10, 1989, 107–27.

The Relevance of Catholic Social Teaching in Poland, especially during the Socialist Period and in the Rise of the Solidarity Movement

Maria Libiszowska-Zoltkowska

There are two kinds of anniversaries. Some bring back to life – for a brief moment – historical facts which, as a rule, remain drowned in the darkness of the distant past and bear no relation to the present. Others do not so much appeal to our collective memory of an event as seem to point out its vitality and presence, in spite of the dominance of the historical aspect of the event.

When – after one hundred years – we analyse the problem of the actuality of the main ideas of *Rerum Novarum* and of its inspiring influence on the present political, economic and mental changes in Poland, we should bear in mind the historical context of the origins of the encyclical. We should also recognize that the present social doctrine which has been functioning through the teachings of the church is being shaped by present conditions, including the situation of Catholic Poland: the motherland of Pope John Paul II. Nowadays there is no single solution in the spirit of Catholic social teaching. On the contrary, there are many possible solutions, depending on time and place. When voicing its ethical and social principles, the church appeals, first of all, to lay Catholics, their involvement and initiative. In addition to the official trend, the involvement of lay Catholics constitutes another trend in Catholic social thought.

Both these trends attempt to define themselves in relation to the major problems of the present situation in Poland. The attitude of the Polish episcopate to socialism has moved from open disapproval to a forced acceptance. The social role of the church in Poland and the influence of its teaching may be regarded in terms of three periods. The first period covers the years after the Second World War and the following period up to the end of the 1960s. The second period covers the 1970s. The last was initiated by the papal election of Cardinal Wojtyla. Until the end of the 1960s Catholic social teaching was practically non-existent in official intellectual life. It was fought against by the régime as an ideologically harmful interpretation and evaluation of social facts, because it competed with Marxist interpretation and evaluation. Restrictions went so far that academic handbooks for the Catholic University in Lublin had to be printed abroad and published under pen-names.

When the Communists seized power in Poland after the Second World War, the Catholic church faced a new unprecedented situation with which it had to cope. The social role of the church was determined, first of all, by the depth of the religious faith of the majority of the nation. This faith not only become a motivating factor for fairly regular attendance at religious rituals, but also gave moral support to social activities. The situation of the church and the status of the faithful were doubly paradoxical. On the one hand, religion was so deeply ingrained in the national history that it was impossible to impose a materialistic ideology on the nation, and the new rule was very much aware of that. On the other hand, the Catholic intelligentsia realized that it was impossible to promulgate Catholic principles of social life, in opposition to the Marxists.

The consolidation of the Communist régime during the early post-war years was accompanied by propaganda which discounted religion and by attempts to limit the activities of the church. The propaganda, which was as a rule primitive, presented the church as an institution which for ages had supported exploitation of the masses and opposed democracy and progress. So the church faced a serious dilemma: either to defend itself against the rule of the state, which was trying to eliminate it from social life, or to defend its values for the sake of the nation. Parallel to the repressions directed against the church, the Catholic press was persecuted. Circulation was limited, and the interference of censorship seriously hampered the possibilities of publishing basic texts. In this situation, the church defended its stand from the pulpits, communicating with the faithful not only by sermons but also by pastoral letters. An analysis of the content of these letters clearly shows that they focussed mainly on the defence of the faith against attacks from atheism.

Psychologically, the negative attitude of the authorities towards the church and the faithful was manifested in an increase in the importance of personal decisions to participate in religious rites, or more generally, in active church membership. Those who made up their minds were actually prepared for an authentic membership and not merely a formal one.

A church marriage or the christening of a child could harm careers. In other circumstances, the special emphasis on the regular participation of the faithful in the Holy Mass and other religious practices, with the simultaneous minimizing of other factors of Christian life, might be seen as the supremacy of a devotional attitude to religion over an intellectual approach. Yet during those years in Poland, this approach was rooted in a conscious choice of tactics for defending the faith against secularization and for shaping of a sense of unity with church organization. Atheism was particularly threatening to the young. Catechism courses organized by the church were expected to counteract this threat. The growth of religious instruction in parishes and the increase of educational influence on the young people seeking contact with the church had a socially positive effect in that it led to a rejection of the atheistic model of life. The church taught respect for the truth, and defied ideological manipulation of national history.

The years 1953–56 were particularly difficult for the Polish church, because of the arrest and detention of the Primate, S. Wyszyński. The régime intended this as a means of weakening the position of the church, but in fact it had the opposite effect. A myth of the imprisoned spiritual leader of the nation was born. During the 1956 workers' strikes which brought about national opposition to the régime, the question of freeing the Primate appeared as the top priority among the demands. Shouts of 'Free the Primate' were heard during all the political parades and public meetings. The actual freeing of the Primate was interpreted by the nation as the first step towards an improvement in church-state relationships, and also as a sign of the normalization of religious life. The immediate effect was the revival of various religious activities. The silence of the Catholic press came to an end: new periodicals appeared. In addition to *Znak* and *Tygodnik Powszechny*, which were suspended in 1953, a new monthly *Więź* was founded in 1958. All of them were edited and published by Catholic intelligentsia. It is from this milieu that the Catholic parliamentary group 'Znak' has been recruited since 1957.

In the period under discussion only the church defended the values and principles generally accepted by the whole nation, and it was the only spokesman of the public opinion which could not be voiced otherwise. The official press, which was hampered and censored, and also lacked social approval, could not possibly perform that function. The struggle for independence was carried out in Parliament by the group of Catholic MPs. Their main goal was to voice not only opinions which reflected their personal consciousness, but also views which were inspired by Catholic social teaching. Because of their small number, the Catholic MPs never succeeded in forcing through their own views if they happened to differ from those of the parliamentary majority. Yet their active presence and protests became a symbol of independent thought and opposition to the régime.

In the aftermath of Vatican II, relations between the state and the church changed considerably. The Catholic milieu emphasized the importance of Paul VI's encyclical commemorating the eightieth anniversary of *Rerum Novarum*, *Octogesima Adveniens*, as the document which made it definitely clear that the papacy was no longer supporting any social systems or models. Publications and social teachings of the church in Poland shifted their stress from macro-problems to micro-problems in the sphere of social questions: family, work environment, demographic and population problems, etc. During this period, the social teachings of the episcopate remained traditionally conservative, as was clearly visible when they were set against the modifications introduced by Vatican II and subsequent papal doctrine. The situation is best reflected in Catholic publications.

After 1960, of almost 150 pastoral letters from the episcopate, nearly 50 dealt with social problems, but none of them were taken up by lay Catholic publications. Some periodicals would merely reprint some of the texts of the pastoral letters.

The real inspiration of Catholic writing in Poland came from papal documents, documents of the Vatican Council and other Vatican documents, or from statements of theologians who were generally considered by the church to be in favour of reforms. The Vatican II Constitution inspired volumes of commentaries by 1970. The Polish Catholic intelligentsia received with a certain relief both the papal statements on cooperation between the faithful and non-believers and the generally more liberal attitude towards Catholics who were involved in socialism. It was with respect to these matters that the doctrine of the Polish church hierarchy was highly uncompromising. The inspiration of post-Vatican II papal doctrine was manifested in Polish Catholicism not so much in the formulation of independent social programmes within its framework as in a search for closer contact with the facts of the Polish situation, involving the philosophy of passive acceptance of the socialist régime as an inevitable reality. In papal social doctrine, Catholic circles found a pragmatic approach to progress, acceptance of natural values of the changes in the world, and therefore resignation to a situation which could not be revoked. Under the influence of post-Vatican II revaluations, and also because of the relaxation of the anti-church policy in Poland, the attitude of the episcopate also became less rigid.

In 1971 when writing about the Primate, S. Wyszyński, Cardinal Wojtyla pointed out that 'when facing the Marxist social system, he is a spokesman of Catholic social teachings, yet with all openness, with an eagerness to see truth and goodness wherever they can be found'. Primate Wyszyński gave priority to the well-being of the nation over the particular interests of the church. In the 1978 'St John's Day Homily' he expressed his wish to seek points of convergence rather than divergencies:

> Poland is a territory on which the Christian and materialistic ideologies meet. It is not always possible to overcome doctrinal differences, and it does not seem fully feasible. Yet – as I have said – there is an instructive experience. It is enough to give at one example. Everyone knows today that even in social, economic, professional and religious spheres of life, the morality expressed in the gospel is required . . . What we need is a great change of man, of his personality. It is on this change that the preservation of our moral, cultural, national, social, professional, economic and religious independence depends . . . We can say that religious life has a positive influence on social and public life; that the strivings of the church are not based on enmity, but consist in bringing help and service.

In the 1970s publishing became animated. Many books by foreign authors were translated into Polish. At the same time works by Polish theologians were published. Shorter contributions were replaced with full synthetic studies. This created a new opportunity for educational activities of the church on a mass scale, and helped to stir the social consciousness of the faithful. The church's assessment of human interrelationships, and its awareness that atheistic school education as implemented in secular schools would not be able to counteract negative phenomena, became the reason for Catholic social thought in the 1970s to focus more on questions of work ethics and morality than on problems of economics and social policy. It was assumed that even the best social reforms would not be capable of changing human interrelationships, and that this could only be achieved by Christian ethics. Therefore the role of morality as the factor that can change negative social and economic phenomena was particularly emphasized. It was argued that injustice could be eliminated from social life only through the moral regeneration of the nation. The church actively jointed the campaign against evidences of social pathology, especially alcoholism. It opposed licentiousness and lack of moral discipline. It supported the family.

In the 1970s, the term 'private property' as used in Poland was understood to denote permanent consumer goods such as a house, land, an apartment; thus it referred to property and not capital. Talk of the right 'to own certain material property' did not include the means of production. Work was the right to property. The question of work was discussed in the context of religious values. Human work became the subject of both theoretical Catholic publications and works of more pragmatic and interventional nature. Catholic periodicals began to publish many articles searching for remedies against negative social phenomena, i.e. simulated work, absenteeism, and the devaluation of work as a mark of social status. Phenomena contributing to the pathology of work were also pointed out. Accusations were aimed at the principles of the socialist system, bad organization of labour, and the atheization of society. Bad organization of labour as well as the system of hierarchical subordination of posts without personal responsibility for decisions are not conducive to conscientious and honest work. Many workers considered their own work a waste of materials and their own efforts.

John Paul II saw the problem very clearly:

A working person desires not only an adequate payment but also such possibilities in the process of production itself that would make him feel that even when working for others, he is at the same time working for himself. This sense is smothered in a system of excessive bureaucratic centralization, in which a working person feels more like a small cog in a huge machine, which is steered from above, he feels more like an ordinary tool for production, an object rather than an authentic subject of work endowed an individual initiative . . . One has to do everything to make it possible that even in this system a person could retain the feeling that he works for himself (*Laborem Exercens*, 15).

The absence of possibilities for improving one's fate were not incentive to activity. A sense of frustration and the vision of work and its organization as an unproductive waste of workers' efforts, combined with economic crisis, brought about a rebellion against the system which was directed against the worker, the system that offered so many promises for the workers and never fulfilled their hopes. It succeeded in making the workers not a well-off leading class but a poor proletariat. Workers supported by peasants and intelligentsia stopped the course of history, but before that, they experienced a predicament that had been envisaged by Leo XIII. He warned:

And such interference is not only unjust, but is quite certain to harass and disturb all classes of citizens, and to subject them to odious and intolerable slavery. It would open the door to envy, to evil speaking, and to quarrelling; the sources of wealth would themselves run dry, for no one would have any interest in exerting his talents or his industry; and that ideal equality of which so much is said would, in reality, be the levelling down of all to the same condition of misery and dishonour (*Rerum Novarum*, 12).

Leo XIII appointed the workers to play the role of the motive power in the process of achieving a desired social order. He saw them as the most harmed and most directly exposed to injustice and therefore as having the greatest moral right to oppose the social order which was evil. However, workers themselves, while suffering wrongs, cannot articulate them.

They need a union which will help them share their fate; they need group solidarity. The Polish workers won such an union. Leo XIII made the church and (in the context of Polish situation) the intelligentsia responsible for the awakening of workers' consciousness, for giving them back their personal pride and dignity.

They have taken up the cause of the working man, and have striven to make both families and individuals better off . . . We see men of eminence meeting together for discussion, for the promotion of united action, and for practical work. Others, again, strive to unite working people of various kinds into associations, help them with their advice and their means, and enable them to obtain honest and profitable work (*Rerum Novarum*, 41).

In Poland, without the active help of the intelligentsia, the working movement would not have been able to play the historical role it did. In order to implement principles of social injustice the solidarity movement was born.

In order to implement social solidarity . . . one requires newer and newer forms of solidarity of working people and also solidarity with working people. Solidarity should always be present in places where there is social degradation of the worker, where there is exploitation and increasing areas of poverty.

These are the teachings of John Paul II in the encyclical *Laborem Exercens* (8). The ethos of the solidarity of working people to defend the meaning and value of work, which has been brought close to the Poles by John Paul II, became an opportunity for the changes in Poland.

The Solidarity movement in Poland grew out of rebellion and hope: it was a protest against bad economic conditions, increasing poverty and the degradation of work. It was a protest in defence of human rights and dignity. The hope was built up by a vision of better organization of work (the ideal of a self-governing society), the awareness of a universal unification of society in common ideas and the collective identification of dangers, and – first of all – by the moral support of Pope John Paul II. The establishment of an identity based on the idea of solidarity, helped by the power of hope and Catholic faith, was the reason why religious overtones penetrated public life, and religious symbols joined the national and patriotic ones. The authority of church leaders became involved in the search for solutions to the most urgent social problems, and the leaders in question took upon themselves the role of advisers and mediators.

In answering the challenge in defence of justice, the church offered Christian ethics in opposition to seductive concepts of overcoming the limitations of enmity. Firm and diplomatic mediations carried out by the church with the aim of preserving social peace resulted in a dialogue which ended the conflict between the régime and the society. The positive presence of the church in social changes in Poland, the fact that both the society and the authorities turned to it for support, is a constructive answer to methods proposed by Leo XIII:

> For no practical solution of this question will ever be found without the assistance of Religion and the Church . . . all the striving of men will be vain if they leave out the church. It is the church that proclaims from the Gospel those teachings by which the conflict can be brought to an end, or at least made far less bitter (*Rerum Novarum*, 13).

'Solidarity' has turned to the church, seeking in it not only social power but also Catholic social teaching. The élite of Catholic intelligentsia played an important role in the formation of the movement. The same élite has for years participated in the development of Catholic social teaching in Poland. Tadeusz Mazowiecki (now the prime minister of Poland), the editor-in-chief of *Więź* (the leading Catholic monthly since 1958), was the closest adviser to Lech Wałesa. The programme of Solidarity, as it was announced in 1981, defined itself as a movement that grew out of the protest of Polish society which over thirty years had experienced violation of human and citizen rights, and as a protest against discrimination for non-Communist beliefs and against economic exploitation. It was an economic and moral protest against socialist rule. As its basic values 'Solidarity' assumed justice, democracy, truth, the rule of law, dignity, and liberty of conscience. The values were defined 'in accordance with the principles of Christian ethics'. 'A new incentive for our activities,' the programme says, 'comes from John Paul II's encyclical on human work. Solidarity as a mass organization of working people is a movement of moral regeneration of the nation.' When fighting for the rights for the working people, the strikers of 1980 also won some rights for the church. As a result, the church got permission to build new churches; it was allowed to perform religious rites in hospitals, in the army, etc.; and it was also given access to the radio (broadcasts of Sunday Mass).

The phenomenon of Polish Catholicism is not limited to the statistical figure of almost 90% faithful. It consists, first of all, in the position of the church (episcopate) among the political powers deciding the fate of a communist country. The position of the church in a Catholic nation of a country with an anti-religious political system forced on it from the outside was extremely complex from the very beginning, and required perspicacity in political judgment as well as diplomacy in action. In the light of recent history (over forty years), the church has not only strengthened its position as a religious institution but, more importantly, is victorious, as its social teachings suppressed and eliminated Marxism.

In highly industrialized Western countries – according to their sociologists – religion has become less and less a national matter; it has become a private and conscious choice of a way of life. The situation is totally reversed in Poland. Religion is increasingly becoming a public value, which is manifested in the increasing number of pro-religious declarations, mass participation in communal cultic practices, the sacralization of public life, and the growth of the social authority of the church and the political role of the episcopate. On the other hand, its influence on private lives seems to be less successful.

Reception of Catholic Social Teaching among Christian Feminists

Maria Riley

Introduction

Tracing the receptivity toward Catholic social teaching by women who are Catholic and feminist is fraught with difficulties. First of all there is minimal scientific data to illustrate either receptivity or non-receptivity to the church's social teaching on the part of the Catholic community as a whole. Secondly, delineating the feminists within the community becomes a matter of subjective judgment unless a person or organization has adopted that term as a self-definition. Moreover, even the term feminist is not without some confusion. Feminism, contrary to popular perception, is not a monolithic ideology, but a rich amalgam of various ideologies, movements, groups and organizations, not all of which are in complete accord.[1]

However, there is evidence of a consistent, even passionate, commitment to justice and peace among groups of women in the church, many of whom would define themselves as feminist. How much this commitment to justice and peace has been informed by the church's 'official' social teaching is less clear, but its influence cannot be denied. This article will explore the question of Catholic feminist women's relationship to Catholic social thought from a theoretical and a practical perspective. In the first part of the article I will explore some critical questions that feminist analysis raises for Catholic social thought, and in the second I will examine some Catholic women's organizations engaged in the church's mission of justice and peace. The focus of the article will be on the experience of feminist Catholic women in the United States.

The question of how influential Catholic social teaching is and has been in the formation of the Catholic community is foundational to this inquiry. A recent commentary on this body of teaching calls it the 'best kept secret' of the Catholic church.[2] It can be argued that Catholic social teaching has for the most part been the concern of academics and professionals in the church. It has also been a part of the curriculum of Catholic high schools and colleges. But how much of its content has informed parish life and the lives of Catholics in general is unclear.[3]

Certainly within the Catholic community there have always been efforts to help the poor, but how that mission of charity translates into work for social justice is questionable. The consternation among some members of the Catholic community when the US bishops wrote the pastorals on peace and on the US economy attests to the lack of understanding within the community of the relationship between faith and justice. A consistent demand from a significant number of Catholics was that the bishops should stay out of politics and return to spiritual questions. Certainly, the American commitment to the separation of church and state was an issue in the complaint. But the deeper issue for many in the community was the challenge to understand the religious dimension of politics and economics in daily life, to move from a privatized faith to a socially responsible life of faith.

For feminists within the community the question is further blurred by the overall feminist critique of the patriarchy which shapes the church's life, structure, liturgical and sacramental celebrations, language, canon law and magisterial teaching – including its social teaching. Feminists question how seriously to take Catholic social teaching when the institutional church itself refuses to address fundamental questions of justice within its own life and structure.

Feminist analysis of Catholic social teaching

Feminism as a social theory is shaped by two fundamental approaches: gender analysis and a liberation motif. Gender analysis adds the gender lens to all social theories and structures, directing particular attention to women's experience. It challenges social theories that purport to be universally applicable to the human person, but does not address the particularities of individual experience, especially those defined by gender. It identifies the different experiences of women and men as critical to understanding social dynamics and social structures.

By using gender as a critical lens of analysis, feminism not only reveals the pervasiveness of patriarchy in social structures but also identifies domination as a central problem in all social dynamics and structures. Domination takes many forms, including that of men over women, the white race over all others, the rich over the poor, humans over creatures.

Among feminists, liberation from these various structures of domination becomes the primary aspiration and motivation for resistance and transformation, starting with the transformation of patriarchy but not limited to that dimension.

Given this focus, the encounter of feminism with Catholic social teaching is ambiguous. Where it finds common cause in the affirmation of the human person and the struggle against structures of injustice, feminism both embraces and is enriched by Catholic social teaching. However, feminism also brings a 'hermeneutic of suspicion' to any body of social theory that has been developed without women's participation and perspective. Therefore, a feminist analysis of Catholic social teaching would question its methodology, ethical foundation and content.

Methodology

In *Sollicitudo Rei Socialis*, John Paul II speaks of the church's three-fold approach to developing social teaching: 1. its 'principles of reflection'; 2. its 'criteria of judgment'; and 3. its 'basic directives for action' (no.3). The first feminist question is: Who defines these principles, criteria and directives? From where do they come? Historically women's voices and experience have been absent from the development of all official church teaching.

From a feminist perspective, this absence of women's contribution is an essential flaw in the methodology of developing Catholic social teaching and paves the way for an inherently patriarchal bias. The inclusion of women's – and other marginalized – voices in the framing of Catholic social teaching is essential if it is to reflect the universalism to which it aspires. This perspective arises from two fundamental insights of feminism: 1. how a person arrives at a particular perspective powerfully influences that perspective; and 2. who is included and who is excluded in the process shapes the content of the analysis.[4] The narrow range of people who have shaped the content of official Catholic social teaching to date certainly limits the scope of its 'principles of reflection'.

Feminist theory would also take issue with the deductive method used in Catholic social teaching to arrive at its universal principles and their concrete applications. Shaped by a liberation motif, feminist theory begins with experience and develops a critical analysis of structures and relationships which then shapes its liberation agenda. From these perspectives Catholic social teaching is flawed, not only in its methodology but also in its analysis.

Ethical Foundation

In writing *Rerum Novarum*, Leo XIII identified natural law as the foundation for shaping the 'criteria of judgment' for the church's reflection on social issues. According to this ethical approach, we are to seek in the nature of things the laws of their proper functioning. For example, through its reflecting on the nature of the human person, Catholic social teaching arrives at its principles of the dignity of the individual and the social nature of human persons.

In general, feminist analysis would accept a form of ethical reflection that starts with human experience, particularly women's experience. However, who interprets that experience and the criteria used would be an issue. These questions open out the complexity of feminist frameworks. The foundations of any given feminist ethic would have to be analysed within the various ideological streams of contemporary feminism – liberal, cultural, Marxist, socialist and radical. However, in the context of this article I am focusing on feminists of the Catholic tradition, so I will presume a degree of acceptance of natural law reflection.

Several questions emerge when a Catholic feminist addresses the natural law ethic. Three of which are key when looking at feminism and Catholic social thought. Whose experience is considered normative for the human? How biologically determined are the reflections? Is the goal of this reflection to discover universal moral norms rooted in a static, essentialist intellectual framework or to discover in human experience the potential to grow, change and re-create human society in more just and life-giving structures? These questions follow the two foundational principles of feminist social theory – gender analysis and liberation aspirations.

Content

In an examination of the Catholic social documents through the lens of these questions, inherent ambiguities and, at times, contradictions are revealed. At these points, Catholic feminists take issue with this body of teaching.

While Catholic social teaching is consistently clear on the dignity and rights of the human person, its view of woman is clearly shaped by a kind of natural law biological determinism. When women are addressed in the documents, the references are clearly shaped by the position that because a woman is capable of bearing children, her nature is defined by that function, and her primary vocation and responsibility is shaped by that nature. This view of woman remains consistent throughout the body of social teaching. In 1891, Leo XIII writes,

Finally, it is not right to demand of a woman or a child what a strong adult man is capable of doing or would be willing to do . . . Certain occupations are less fitted for women, who are intended by nature for work of the home – work indeed which especially protects modesty in women and accords by nature with the education of children and the well-being of the family (*Rerum Novarum*, 60).

In 1963, John XXIII writes,

> Women have the right to working conditions in accordance with their requirements and their duties as wives and mothers (*Pacem et Terris*, 19).

Almost twenty years later, after the historical shift in consciousness by women and about women, John Paul II repeats the same basic message. He recognizes that changes have occurred, but he insists that by their nature women are primarily mothers:

> Experience confirms that there must be a social re-evaluation of the mother's role, of the toil connected with it and of the need that children have for care, love and affection in order that they may develop into responsible, morally and religiously mature and psychologically stable persons. It will redound to the credit of society to make it possible for a mother – without inhibiting her freedom, without psychological or practical discrimination, and without penalizing her as compared with other women – to devote herself to taking care of her children and educating them in accordance with their needs, which vary with age. Having to abandon these tasks in order to take up paid work outside the home is wrong from the point of view of the good of society and of the family when it contradicts or hinders these primary goals of the mission of the mother.

> The true advancement of women requires that labour should be structured in such a way that women do not have to pay for their advancement by abandoning what is specific to them and at the expense of the family, in which women as mothers have an irreplaceable role (*Laborem Exercens*, 19).

What is striking in these documents is the failure to recognize the social role, vocation and mission of fatherhood. When fathers are mentioned, it is primarily in an economic context. For example, Leo XIII writes:

> It is a most sacred law of nature that the father of a family see that his offspring are provided with all the necessities of life and nature even

prompts him to desire to provide and to furnish his children, who, in fact reflect and in a sense continue his person, with the means of decently protecting themselves against harsh fortune in the uncertainties of life . . . As already noted, the family like the State is by the same token a society in the strictest sense of the term, and it is governed by its own proper authority, namely by that of the father (*Rerum Novarum*, 20).

This economic role of the father is consistently reiterated under the theme of the 'family wage', a concept that presupposes an employed father, a mother in the home and dependent children. This ideal of the so-called 'traditional family', which is patriarchal in structure, is a reflection of the middle-class family that emerged during the Industrial Revolution. It has never been a universal experience of families. Poor and working-class women have always had to work outside the home. It does not reflect the reality of today's post-industrialized societies. Nor is it an accurate representation of families in more traditional, pre-industrialized or industrializing countries. The question of whose experience is normative and therefore the basis of natural law reflection is critical here.

This biologically determined view of women also becomes evident in the documents when they purport to be speaking of human nature and human rights. Women's ability to participate fully in all arenas of the human community is consistently being circumscribed by their so-called nature. For example, in *Gaudium et Spes*, the council fathers write:

In every group or nation, there is an ever-increasing number of men and women who are conscious that they themselves are the artisans and the authors of the culture of their community . . . Women are now employed in almost every area of life. It is appropriate that they should be able to assume their full proper role in accordance with their own nature (55, 60).

In 1971, Paul VI repeats the same perspective in *Octogesima Adveniens*:

Similarly, in many countries a charter for women which would put an end to an actual discrimination and would establish relationships of equality in rights and of respect for their dignity is the object of study and at times of lively demands. We do not have in mind that false equality which would deny the distinctions laid down by the Creator himself and which would be in contradiction with women's proper role, which is of such capital importance, at the heart of the family as well as within society. Development of legislation should on the contrary be directed to protecting her proper vocation and at the same time recognizing her independence as a person, and her equal rights to participate in cultural, economic, social and political life (13).

In this passage Paul VI does identify an issue that has become crucial in feminist policy debates. The issue is how to realize in theory, policy and practice both the radical equality and the fundamental difference between women and men. The debate is about the limits of equality, the meaning of difference and their implications in framing social policy and strategy.

The code-words of the debate are 'special treatment' versus 'equal treatment', and 'gender-specific laws' versus 'gender-neutral laws'. The debate is about how to treat women in public policy. Should there be 'special treatment'/'gender-specific laws'? Or should there be 'equal treatment'/'gender-neutral laws'? What are the implications of each in assuring equality for women? How to deal with pregnancy in social policy is the core of the debate. The ideal sought by both sides is to insure recognition of and accommodation to women's special needs at the time of pregnancy and childbirth, and to protect women's hard-won and still incomplete equality of opportunity and participation in public life.[5]

In *Octogesima Adveniens*, Paul VI recognizes the complexity of the issue, but feminists would challenge his insistence on women's 'proper vocation' as limiting and informed by the kind of biologic determinism that shapes Catholic social thought *vis-à-vis* women. Catholic social teaching's ability to contribute to this significant debate on the future shape of human institutions is significantly limited by this determinism.

From this analysis of the content of the documents it is clear that the framework of natural law used is shaped by a patriarchal bias. Man, that is the male person, is considered normative when the 'human person' is defined. Woman is consistently dealt with through the particular lens of her 'proper nature', and consequently her access and freedom in the exercise of the full realization of human rights as understood within the body of teaching is limited. Woman is too often dealt with as an exception to the norms established for the human. Furthermore, this limited view of woman – and therefore also of man – is fixed and static within a world view of 'proper roles', which limits the vision and scope of searching for more just and mutual structures in human relationships and institutions.

The feminist 'hermeneutic of suspicion' in approaching Catholic social teaching is confirmed by this analysis of its methodology, ethical foundation and content. It can be identified as patriarchal for three reasons: 1. it is written by men, primarily about men; 2. its bias is androcentric, that is, it assumes that man, in this case, white, Western man, is normative for the human; and 3. when women are included, they are defined from this male point of view. The patriarchy of its methodology inevitably shapes the interpretation of natural law and its application in content.

Women and the church's mission for justice

The second approach to the question of how women who are Catholic and feminist respond to Catholic social teaching is to examine several Catholic women's organizations in the United States who are engaged in the work for justice and peace and recognize this engagement as a faith commitment. Through interviews and examination of documentation of these organizations some general conclusions can be drawn. The information provided is not intended to be comprehensive, nor are the organizations described necessarily representative of all the groups who work on issues of justice and peace. The choice of organizations has been directed by three considerations: they are women's organizations; they are predominantly Catholic; and they have a history of work for justice and peace.

Religious congregations of women have had a profound and significant role in shaping the justice and peace agenda in the United States Catholic community. Over the past twenty five years, in addition to their congregational work for justice, they have committed personnel, resources and financial support to innumerable justice and peace organizations, groups and efforts. Without this commitment, the justice and peace movement of the church would not have the vitality it has in the United States.

From where did this extraordinary commitment come? Its roots are in the Sister Formation programme of the 1950s, but the flowering came in the extraordinary ecclesial and social ferment of the 1960s. The impact of the Second Vatican Council cannot be overestimated. It not only called religious congregations to rediscover their original charism and renew that charism for the contemporary world, but also opened the whole church to a much wider engagement with the critical issues of the age. The two Council documents *Perfectae Caritatis* and *Gaudium et Spes* were key factors in directing the renewal process of most congregations in the United States.

The consistent call in official church documents for 'a special option for the poor' has had a profound formational influence on the development of community life and mission. In *Octogesima Adveniens* (1971), Paul VI specifically asked, 'How can the call of the poor find an echo in the lives of religious?' (18). That same year the Synod of Bishops issued *Justice in the World*, with its insistence that, 'Action on behalf of justice and participation in the transformation of the world fully appear to us a constitutive dimension of the preaching of the Gospel . . .'(6). According to Marie Augusta Neal, SND, 'By 1980, this question was the dominant one in the renewal chapters of many religious congregations of women . . .'[6]

But Vatican II and the call for renewal were not the only influences operative in religious congregations since the 1960s. During that period of time the liberation movements have changed the context of our understanding of the church's mission for justice. Among women, the key liberation movement has, of course, been feminism. The introduction of feminism into religious life has created ambiguity and tension within the community and in some instances in its relationship to the official church. While to my knowledge no congregation would define itself as feminist, most congregations have a significant number of women who would define themselves as feminist and who exert leadership within the communities.

Leadership Conference of Women Religious (LCWR), the umbrella organization for women's congregations in the United States, whose mandate is ' . . . to promote a developing understanding and living of religious life . . .', has been a consistent leader in the promotion of the justice agenda within religious communities. Its 1989–1994 goals include solidarity with women for the transformation of social and ecclesial structures, effective action for justice, and work to eliminate the sin of racism (LCWR Brochure, np,nd). In addition, the language of the goals reflects a feminist perspective, calling for styles of leadership consonant with its members experience as women; a theology of religious life shaped by the experience of women in the church; and calls for mutuality, liberation and harmony. While LCWR does not explicitly identify itself as feminist, it is clearly informed with a feminist perspective on relationships, authority and liberation.

The Grail can in some ways be viewed as a Catholic woman's lay alternative to canonical religious life. Founded in Holland in 1921, the Grail evolved from an idealistic youth movement to an international group of Catholic laywomen committed to 'lead the way in the development of the apostolate of women'.[7] In its beginning the Grail vision was informed with the traditional Catholic action concept – the participation of the laity in the apostolate of the hierarchy. Catholic social teaching was always a strong influence on the Catholic action movement. However, by the late 1960s the Grail defined itself as politically feminist with a clear commitment to women's rights, and therefore the Grail's right to self-definition and direction. While retaining its original identity as a group of lay women rooted in the Christian faith and called 'to participate in the transformation of the world', the Grail now attends to the task 'even more aware of the relations of domination and submission which are embedded in our social, political and economic structures' (quoted in Weaver, 126). Today the Grail is informed by its two historical roots, Catholic social teaching and feminist liberation theology, out of which the women of the Grail continue to form a new synthesis for action and reflection for justice and peace.

During the 1970s several autonomous women's organizations were founded by members of religious congregations: NARW (National Assembly of Religious Women), *Network*, A National Catholic Social Justice Lobby, and WOC (Women's Ordination Conference). While the membership in these organizations was initially primarily women in religious communities, that is no longer true as the organizations have sought to bond with laywomen and men. These organizations define themselves as feminist.

NARW, founded in 1970, is clearly feminist, identifying itself as an organization for Catholic feminist women 'to provide a forum and voice for women of faith to respond to justice issues within church and society' (NARW promotional material np, nd). While NARW does not overtly identify Catholic social teaching in its documents, its roots in the renewal process of religious communities would include that reality. Today, its language of self-description is strongly shaped by both feminist analysis and the liberation motif. Its approach is to examine and respond 'to issues through the specific lens of women's concerns'; it 'rejects competition among organizations and understands coalition-building and networking as basic to the development of its own strength and vision' (ibid.). It also sees itself as a forum for women's empowerment. Its arena of work is both the church and the society.

Network was founded in 1971 from a vision of bias for the poor. Its self-definition and focus is clearly feminist: '*Network* supports issues that encourage equal relations between persons and among nations – a feminist, non-sexist view – and one that rejects all patterns of relationships that are based on domination and submission' (*Network* brochure np, nd). It also identifies Catholic social teaching as the basis of its values: '*Network* is rooted in the tradition of Catholic social teaching and Gospel values. It seeks to be faithful to the encyclicals, Vatican II and to the voice of the church, in the United States, such as the "Call to Action" and the bishops' pastorals on peace and the US economy' (ibid.). Furthermore, in its educational outreach, *Network* has worked to make Catholic social teaching more universally known throughout the church. However, it also brings a feminist critique to the documents as part of its contribution to the evolution of Catholic social thought. While the focus of *Network*'s work is social policy and the political process in the United States, it is also part of the larger movement for justice for women in the church.

WOC (Women's Ordination Conference) was founded after the First Women's Ordination Conference in Detroit (1976). While its primary focus remains the ordination of women, it understands that goal within the context of a church transformed beyond patriarchy and not just within a 'add women and stir' process. Hence its agenda moves beyond the single question of ordination to include the empowerment of women in the church and society. Its work reflects a gender analysis and the liberation motif. WOC calls upon the tradition of Catholic social teaching in seeking justice for women in the church. In particular it reminds the hierarchy of their statement in *Justice in the World*: 'While the Church is bound to give witness to justice, she recognizes that anyone who ventures to speak to people about justice must first be just in their eyes' (3).

Two other groups of women in religious communities founded organizations to address the specific injustice they encountered in both their congregations and in the church: The National Black Sisters Conference and Las Hermanas.

The National Black Sisters Conference was founded in 1968 to counter racism in the church, in religious communities and in society. Its origin was in the Civil Rights Movement of the 1960s in the United States. According to Gwynette Proctor SND, Executive Director, the National Black Sisters Conference was founded out of a void of justice, not in response to Catholic social teaching (Interview, 27 December 1990). It was founded to develop the leadership of African American religious women and to provide a voice and locus of action to confront racism. The United States pastoral letter, *Brothers and Sisters to Us All: A Pastoral Letter on Racism* (1979), is the most relevant expression of Catholic social teaching that informs the work of the Conference, but its very existence attests to the failure of Catholic social teaching to shape the life of the Catholic community.

While the National Black Sisters Conference does not define itself as feminist, it does call itself womanist, the word first used by Alice Walker to describe the African American women's movement. In using the word womanist, the African American women identify their liberation process as women affirming women with respect for 'who the person is, what the person is and whose the person is', that is, who is the primary cultural and racial community to which that person belongs (Proctor). This process aims to be culture-sensitive to all women, recognizing cultural differences and values and committed to the survival and wholeness of all people (Proctor). The womanist movement identifies itself as being distinct from mainline US feminism, which it sees as dominated by white women and too narrowly focused on promoting women, without a sufficient sensitivity to or even knowledge of the effects of racism on women and men.

Las Hermanas was founded by two Chicana women religious who had begun to encounter resistance in their congregations and in the dioceses to their work for social justice in education among the Mexican American people. The dynamic for their work was the Chicano Movement, and they wanted to organize Mexican American women in religious communities to accompany the people in their struggle. They also believed that the opportunities they enjoyed in religious communities had given them skills and talents that would be of service to the people, but they needed support in their efforts to move their congregations to support their work and commitment. The founders of Las Hermanas sought to link the political and religious power of the people (Interview with Yolanda Tarango, Executive Director to Las Hermanas, 17 January 1991).

In its twenty year history Las Hermanas has evolved from a movement of Mexican American sisters to include all Latina women in the United States, with a specific focus on the needs and aspirations of Latina women in the church and society. By 1975 it was clearly embracing a feminist perspective, but as the movement matured, Las Hermanas was moving towards a self-defined understanding of feminism. According to Yolanda Tarango, it remains feminist in principle but wants to distance itself from some of the white feminist movement, which, it feels, does not take sufficient note of race, culture or class in its gender analysis. Many in Las Hermanas are now using the word *mujerista* rather than 'feminist' (interview, 17 January 1991).

Las Hermanas looks primarily to the documents of Medellin and Puebla for its understanding of Catholic social teaching, but it is also influenced by Latin American liberation theology. The official papal documents and even the US bishops' pastoral letters are less well known (Tarango).

During the 1980s, Womenchurch emerged as a loosely organized movement that draws together predominantly feminist women within the church in the United States. Its primary goal is the empowerment of women to achieve justice for women in church and society. It is clearly informed by both a gender perspective and a feminist liberation motif. Like other feminist organizations, it would look to Catholic social teaching to support its demands for justice, but be critical of the patriarchy that informs that body of teaching, as well as the patriarchy that shapes the institutional church.

The most difficult group of women to identify are the lay women in the church who do not have the institutional base religious communities to provide organizational power and financial resources. Some lay women are part of NARW, *Network*, WOC, Las Hermanas and Womenchurch, but the vast majority of women are not connected with any organization. The National Council of Catholic Women (NCCW) is the officially recognized Catholic organization of women in the United States. It is structurally related to the National Conference of Catholic Bishops, the United States Catholic Conference and local dioceses. According to Annette Kane, Executive Director, Catholic social teaching shapes its positions and programmes initiated from the national office, but it is difficult to judge how local organizations or members respond. Historically, the NCCW has been more active in service to the needy than in political action for change (interview, 2 January 1991). Likewise, although individual members may be feminist, as an organization NCCW is not feminist, and is perceived by some to be anti-feminist since its lack of support for the Equal Rights Amendment. Furthermore, the NCCW does not represent all Catholic women.

However, within the Catholic community women have traditionally worked for the church's mission, be it the mission of mercy or mission of justice. The Notre Dame study of parish life revealed that 85% of the ministries to the poor, elderly, sick and disabled are carried on by women. Women, likewise, do 85% of the justice and peace work.[8] For feminist women, who recognize that the liberation of women is intrinsic to justice and peace, this commitment has sometimes led to conflict and even separation from parish life. While again there are no statistics, anecdotal evidence abounds.

For example, one group of inventive lay women in Northern Virginia opened the Center for A New Creation as a response to the lack of commitment to the issues of justice both in the church and by the church. Joan Urbanczyk, one of the founders of the Center, said: 'I rejoice when the church speaks, I am discouraged that the church and its people neither hears nor heeds the message' (interview, 28 December 1990). The church's refusal to address women's questions was an important catalyst to the founding of the Center in 1979.

Conclusion

Clearly, among women who are Catholic and feminist, Catholic social teaching has been a formative value. However, feminist analysis and liberation theology has also been critical in forming the women's consciousness and conscience. The women clearly linked their struggle for justice as integral to the church's mission of justice and peace. It is not two struggles, but one. A clear truth has emerged in their lives: unless women take their own liberation seriously, their work for justice for others can be maternalistic and condescending. They also realize that their liberation process is not only about justice for women; it is also about the integrity of the gospel, the authenticity and effectiveness of the church's mission for justice and peace in our day, and the liberation of God from the narrow confines of patriarchy.

Notes

1. For a exploration of the different feminisms that shape the current feminist movement see Maria Riley, *Transforming Feminism*, Kansas City 1989.

2. Peter J. Henriot, Edward P. DeBerri and Michael J. Schultheis, *Catholic Social Teaching: Our Best Kept Secret*, Maryknoll 1988.

3. A 1987 Gallup survey of the reception of the US bishops' pastorals on peace and the US economy revealed the following information. Of the people surveyed, only 29% had heard of or read the peace pastoral; 67% had not read or heard of it; and 5% were unsure. For the pastoral on the US economy, 25% had read or heard of it; 71% had not read or heard of it; and 4% were unsure. Of those who were familiar with the pastorals 57% agreed with the peace pastoral; 29% disagreed; and 14% did not know. 71% agreed with the pastoral on the US economy; 21% disagreed with it; and 8% did not know. In a gender analysis of this data, the survey revealed that 69% of the women survey were in favour of the peace pastoral while only 64% of the men were in favour and 81% of the women surveyed were in favour of the pastoral on the US economy, while only 74% of the men surveyed were in favour (William D'Antonio, James Davidson, Dean Hoge and Ruth Wallace, *American Catholic Laity in a Changing Church*, Kansas City 1989, 166, 171 and 174).

4. Maria Riley, 'Feminist Analysis: A Missing Perspective', *The Logic of Solidarity: Commentaries on Pope John Paul II's Encyclical 'On Social Concern'*, Maryknoll 1989, 189.

5. For more complete analysis of this debate see Lise Vogel, 'Debating Difference: Feminism, Pregnancy and the Workplace', *Feminist Studies* 16.1, (1990), 9–32, and the Center of Concern's *Comments on the Second Draft National Conference of Catholic Bishops' Pastoral Letter – One in Christ Jesus: A Pastoral Response to the Concerns of Women for Church and Society*, Washington, DC 1990.

6. Marie Augusta Neal SND, *From Nuns to Sisters: An Expanding Vocation*, Mystic, CT 1990, 33.

7. Mary Jo Weaver, *New Catholic Women: A Contemporary Challenge to Traditional Religious Authority*, San Francisco 1985, p.120.

8. David C. Leege and Thomas A. Trozzolo, *Participation in Catholic Parish Life: Religious Rites and Parish Activities in the 1980s*, Report 3, Notre Dame Study of Catholic Parish Life, 1985, 7.

Liberation Theology and the Social Teaching of the Church

Ricardo Antoncich

Liberation theology has taken a critical view of the social teaching of the church. This is a general statement and needs to be modified, since there are different strands within liberation theology and different levels of criticism, as well as distinct periods in the social teaching.

Liberation theology has different currents. Within its common concern for the cause of the poor, some affirm the need for analytical instruments taken from the social sciences to uncover and overcome the causes of injustice (Gutiérrez, the brothers Boff), while others look to the humanities as a way of interpreting popular aspirations to liberation (L. Gera, J. C. Scannone). The first group criticize the social teaching of the church; the second do not.

Critiques also take place on different levels. There is absolutely no questioning of the church's right and duty to pronounce on temporal matters; here liberation theology and the *magisterium* are at one. There is recognition of the danger of such pronouncements being contaminated by ideological interests. Liberation theology first raised this suspicion in relation to the social teaching of the church; the *magisterium* then turned the tables by suspecting liberation theology of the same fault, warning about its use of Marxist analysis in two documents from the Congregation for the Doctrine of the Faith, *Libertatis Nuntius* and *Libertatis Conscientia*.

The social teaching can legitimately be criticized for the way it has been interpreted and used. The suspicion that certain texts, such as those defending private property, have been used and understood outside their context and taken as legitimation for moves against much-needed land reforms in some developing countries; the suspicion that some documents, such as the two from the Congregation mentioned above, have been given widespread media coverage while criticisms of liberal capitalism have been silenced – these are based on real facts and are not arbitrary.

In this article I want to show, first, how a liberation theology in contact with Marxist criticism can shed light on some aspects of the social teaching; second, how recent documents of the *magisterium* have themselves stressed points of convergence between the social teaching and liberation theology.

1. Liberation theology, Marxism and social teaching

Marxism, with its critique of ideology as camouflage and of the role of religion within ideology, has underlain much of liberation theology's criticism of the social teaching. Paradoxically, however, these criticisms have also encouraged an interpretation of the social teaching of the church that is legitimate, more faithful to the option for the poor and closer to the values of the gospel. While we have to listen to the *magisterium*'s warnings about the use of Marxism, we cannot avoid noticing the positive aspects of its influence. I should like to take three major points where its influence has been positive: the meaning of property, the attitude to social conflict, and the unity between faith and justice as a refutation of the critique of religion as alienating.

(a) Social analysis and private property
  Libertatis Nuntius questioned the lack of objectivity of Marxist social analyses. But the *magisterium* does not see itself as competent to judge the scientific worth of social sciences. Therefore this lack of objectivity has to be referred to the area of religious experience, in which the church can legitimately pronounce on the objectivity of a social analysis. Marxist prejudice in seeing religion as a source of human alienation determines the selection of facts that will confirm this prejudice and the omission of others that will contradict it. Here, the warnings in *Libertatis Nuntius* are to the point. But Marxism and its analyses do not deal with religion alone; they insist on the fact that the root cause of the exploitation of labour is private ownership of the means of production. Liberation theology, more sensitive to this critique, emphasizes the need for an interpretation of the church's teaching on property that will show that defending the right to property is not a matter of protecting the selfishness of the wealthy, but the real way of defending the rights of the poor. The social teaching itself has suggestive elements here: (i) the subordination of the right to property to another more basic and primary right, the law of the communal purpose of all earthly goods; (ii) the social function of property, which limits its

individual use and requires taking responsibility for the common good in the use of goods, with the consequent 'social mortgage' spoken of by John Paul II; (iii) the priority of labour over capital and the concept of a just wage, taken as an index of the justness of a particular society (*Laborem Exercens* 19).

In this centenary year of *Rerum Novarum*, we should remember that its first argument in favour of private ownership of the means of production is the worker's right to acquire this, by means of a wage that will enable him to satisfy his consumption needs and acquire property. To be precise, this first argument speaks of the right *to* ownership, the right of those who do not yet have property, rather than the rights *of* ownership, the rights of those who are already owners. Unfortunately, this aspect of the church's social teaching on ownership of the means of production has never been stressed.

(b) Philosophical aspects and social conflict

Libertatis Nuntius also warns against the philosophical aspects of Marxism based on dialectical materialism and its interpretation of conflictivity as a historical necessity. But apart from the metaphysical aspects of Marxist definition of this conflictivity, social conflict exists as an actual fact, as *Laborem Exercens* (11d) recognizes, before its derivation in ideological conflicts. Overcoming the conflict between capital and labour is a necessary task in building a just world. This goal will not be achieved by means of violently imposing the priority of labour over capital through a party or state that appoints itself the representative of the workers. This has been shown by the recent changes that have taken place in Eastern Europe. This does not mean that affirming the priority of labour over capital has ceased to be, as *Laborem Exercens* calls it, a deeply human and Christian task in the face of a system that still upholds another priority: that of capital.

So liberation theology reminds the *magisterium* that warnings about the class struggle must not in any way lead to lack of commitment in the face of the clamour of the poor, or to failure to defend their trampled rights – as indeed *Libertatis Nuntius* (XI) recognizes.

(c) Religion and human alienation

On this third point, liberation theology appears precisely as an argument against the objection to religion as alienation of the people. While Marxism, under the influence of Feuerbach, tried to explain the phenomenon of religion as a mere projection of the exploited seeking to escape the miseries of their historical condition through the promise of other-worldly consolation, liberation theology has been at pains to show that God is not indifferent to their sufferings in this world; that God sent his Son to share in the human condition from within human history, in order to transform it in the way of solidarity, justice and love, in the incipient but historically significant presence of the kingdom of God.

We can here say that if critiques inspired by Marxism can lead to a better presentation of the Christian message, then they have a positive side to them.

2. Toward greater convergence between liberation theology and the social teaching of the church

It must be recognized, too, that the presentation of the social teaching of the church has become clearer and more nuanced, at least partly in order to clear up ambiguities that lend themselves to ideological manipulation. Therefore, its distinct stages need to be emphasized.

One cannot say that the social teaching has been indifferent to the Third World, with the industrialized countries as its sole interlocutor. At least since *Populorum Progressio* and *Mater et Magistra*, such an objection cannot be sustained. John XXIII's teaching on regional and national inequalities, and Paul VI's words on authentic development, brought up to date by John Paul II in *Sollicitudo Rei Socialis*, are proof of a concern not only to deal with the problems of the Third World, but to do so from the standpoint of the poor.

One can no longer say, either, that the *magisterium* shows itself as a universal abstraction, trying to steer Christians' actions in a monolithic way. Since *Octogesima Adveniens*, there has been an insistence on the interpretation local churches must make of universal principles, criteria and norms. The fact that this possibility has often been under-utilized, and the local *magisteria* have been content to quote what has been said by the papal *magisterium*, is a problem that derives not from the *magisterium* itself, but from its interpretation.

On our three points – property, conflict and alienation – the two social encyclicals of John Paul II make a considerable advance.

(a) A better understanding of ownership

With regard to ownership, *Laborem Exercens* sets out the need for labour and capital to be always united and never separate, let alone opposed; the legitimacy of ownership consists in the service it gives to labour. Here the Pope adopts, more clearly than in previous documents of the social *magisterium*, an ethical (the subordinate relationship of the means of production to labour) and non-ideological (private ownership v. social ownership) viewpoint that leaves the door open for different countries to adopt different solutions. He is content to set out the criteria that make both forms of ownership legitimate tools of a just social order, and to denounce how both run the same risk of 'economicism', when a few hands (private or state) control the economy without regard for their legitimate concerns of the workers.

Sollicitudo Rei Socialis also urges application of the teaching on the universal destiny of goods; it asks that surpluses should be shared out, even going into specific details like the moral obligation on the church to sell costly ornaments in order to provide for the urgent needs of the poor (31g), and the moral duty to promote the development of countries that have not yet achieved it.

(b) A deeper vision of social conflict

Laborem Exercens clears up a misunderstanding arising from a mistaken view of one aspect of the social teaching: that by opposing the class struggle, the church is paralysing the people's struggle to defend the rights of the marginalized and the oppressed. John Paul II seeks to uncover a universal human motive in the workers' struggle for their rights: it is not the working class as such, nor its limited rights, that demands radical compromise; it is rather the human values they embody – human activity as the basis of 'being more', of 'being in solidarity'. The actual human group of workers enshrines not only group or class interests, but also an invitation to recognize the value of work performed in solidarity. The response to this invitation produces the movement of 'solidarity of working people and solidarity with working people' (8f). Applied to the church, this is the test of the truth of its faithfulness to Christ in order to be truly 'the church of the poor'. The conflict between capital and labour does not consist only of the opposed interests of two social classes; it appears in the very basis of moral choice, shown in the existence of values that give meaning to human life.

Once the labour-capital conflict is understood in this way, then neutrality is not an option. 'Capital' is here given negative qualities: the quest to have more at the expense of being more, the exclusive concentration on money and profit derived from exploitation of labour – the historical experience of early liberal capitalism and still a permanent temptation to many forms of central or peripheral capitalism. But the Pope is not adopting an attitude of radical mistrust of progress, initiative and competition, of building up capital with a view to future expansion that can benefit labour. Capitalism's perennial 'temptation' can be overcome by subordinating capital to labour; when this is done, capital itself is worthy of respect and appreciation.

Over against a capitalism that can be 'redeemed' stands the value of labour as human self-fulfilment in relation to nature and within the human collectivity. But the positive dimension of work can be 'prostituted' when work loses its human dimension, when it is subject to the sheer interests of capital and, by serving these, becomes exploitative of others' work.

(c) A liberating meaning of the Christian faith

Finally, both John Paul II's social encyclicals take a step forward in answering the Marxist critique of religion. The Pope puts forward a spirituality of work as active commitment to the transformation of this world through production of economic goods and a just social order, a process that corresponds to the will of God and places those who work within the mystery of Christ's redemptive action. In this case, spirituality is not something set apart from immanent human activity, nor is work seen purely as a this-worldly task; both dimensions overlap and the actual work which transforms worldly goods and establishes new forms of human community reveals the plan of creation and redemption, God's work, in which all human beings are invited to collaborate. The fatigue and satisfaction involved in all work-processes and their results evoke the paschal mystery of new life which passed through sacrifice and abnegation.

The concept of the spirituality of work can be broadened and enriched if it is applied not only to the transformation of worldly goods or services to human beings, but to the transformation of the whole of society in the direction of structural justice. If all work has to overcome 'resistances', we have to recognize that 'social resistances' are much more obdurate than physical ones. The selfishness of individual interests opposed to the common good is harder to bend than steel or any other metal. Overcoming such barriers to the promotion of justice is a true social labour that fully deserves to considered as a spirituality.

When the poor, then, try through their organizations and struggles for justice to break down the barriers that stand in the way of this genuine human advancement, they are performing a more social than physical task, and one which has clear repercussions on their sharing in the sufferings of Christ and in his victory in the paschal mystery. When we speak of Christ 'working' in his lifetime, we can limit ourselves to his work as a carpenter in Nazareth, losing sight of his other 'work' as author of the personal and social conversion initiated by the gospel. In this, he did not put forward a theory of society, nor organize an alternative political system, but he did display the religious experience of the Fatherhood of God, which is capable of awakening a conversion to solidarity. The spirituality of work, as expressed in *Laborem Exercens*, has a strong convergence towards the spirituality of liberation, particularly in its stress on reference to the paschal mystery of Christ's suffering and victory.

It is, nevertheless, in *Sollicitudo Rei Socialis*, particularly its chapter 5, that liberation theology finds an even more basic convergence between its own intuitions and the social teaching of the church. Here the Pope speaks of a theological reading of contemporary problems. This is to recognize the basic intuition that all history, human history and salvation history (with necessary distinctions but no separation), is one. The economic, social and political history of humankind is read from the history of salvation, and so grace is proclaimed and sin denounced in the concrete historical actions of imperialism or solidarity. The doctrinal message is not 'elevated' to a metaphysical abstraction, but most incisively applied to very tangible realities. Now nothing could be more convergent with liberation theology than recognizing the presence of sin in the imperialism of powerful nations imposing themselves on weak and poor ones; nothing could be more convergent with liberation theology than recognizing signs of faithfulness to the grace that comes from the Lord of history in solidarity with the poor and oppressed. These two aspects, sin and grace, made present in history, belong to what is most central and valuable in liberation theology. So we can say that chapter 5 of *Sollicitudo Rei Socialis* is real liberation theology done in the very context of the social teaching of the church.

The recent documents from dicasteries of the Holy See, on teaching the social doctrine of the church in seminaries, and on the identity of theologians in the exercise of their ecclesial ministry, while a sign of the present anxieties felt by the hierarchy, are also a recognition of the urgency of these problems and of the importance of the social teaching – long forgotten and marginalized in the formation of priests – and of the need to define the dialogue between theologians and the social sciences with greater accuracy. It is possible that if liberation theology had not existed, these documents would not have seen the light of day.

If it is possible to visualize a future convergence of the *magisterium* and liberation theology, it is important not to forget the initial convergence: liberation theology is strongly tied to the Latin American *magisterium* as expressed at Medellín and Puebla. So it is not a question of parallel *magisteria* of theologians and hierarchy, but of a convergence of charisms and ecclesial functions whose criteria of legitimacy need to be inspired in conversion to the gospel and fidelity to the following of Christ.

Translated by Paul Burns

Communicating Catholic Social Teaching: The Experience of the Church in the United States of America

Dennis P. McCann

Catholic social teaching throughout the twentieth century has had a significant impact on public policy in the United States. Indeed, it is virtually impossible to understand the contours of contemporary American social history without reference to the timely interventions of the National Catholic Welfare Conference (NCWC) and its successor, the United States Catholic Conference (USCC). The 'Bishops' Program of Social Reconstruction' (1919), for example, foreshadowed much of the 'New Deal' legislation implemented during the presidency of Franklin Delano Roosevelt (1933–1945), as the church allied itself with various progressive movements ranging from organized labour to civil rights. Prior to the impact of the recent pastoral letters of the Ntaional Conference of Catholic Bishops (NCCB), the papal encyclical, *Pacem in Terris* (1963), seems to have set the standard for public visibility, as Pope John XXIII's expansive understanding of human rights and his challenging vision of a cooperative international order became the object of intensive study in academic and professional circles, especially those concerned with American foreign policy.

Why and how these previous achievements were so dramatically eclipsed by the public reception of the recent pastoral letters, *The Challenge of Peace* (1983), and *Economic Justice for All* (1986), I hope to analyse in what follows. But the task of communicating Catholic social teaching obviously cannot be reduced to questions of public reception. A concern of how this teaching is developed within the church itself clearly enjoys at least logical priority. Here, for most of this period, however, the scope of influence seems curiously confined to a socially activist clerical élite. Ordinary Catholics who in virtually all other respects were living faithfully within the church were normally uninstructed in the practice of social justice, if not completely ignorant of the contents of this teaching. Even among lay social activists, the typical pattern involved turning for guidance to Catholic social teaching after they had become involved in some progressive movement for social change, and not before. Catholic social teaching within the church did not so much challenge the faithful to commit themselves to social activism as help Catholic social activists to discover the religious and moral bases of their distinctive commitments.

One plausible hypothesis for understanding, among American Catholics, the relatively limited influence of Catholic social teaching prior to Vatican Council II must begin with an assessment of the long-term consequences of the papal condemnations first of the so-called 'Americanist' heresy and later of Modernism. Whatever the immediate occasion of Leo XIII's encyclical *Testem Benevolentiae* (1899), there is no doubt that it served as a pre-emptive strike against an emerging style of public engagement by a local church that had grown to appreciate precisely the pastoral opportunities opened up by a society dedicated to the ideals of democratic pluralism. The visionary yet critical openness to American values preached and practised by Isaac Hecker, John Ireland, Edward McGlynn and numerous others gave way to a more defensive posture that stressed devotionalism in one's personal spirituality and a bare-knuckled pragmatism in the church's social witness. The resulting ecclesial style, known to American Catholic scholars as that of the 'immigrant church', valued the papal encyclicals that formed the backbone of Catholic social teaching mostly for the programmatic support they gave to the trade union movement, and the host of progressive social causes associated with it. Rare indeed, in those days, was any critical discussion of the distinctive vision of human nature and society that informed the papal encyclicals; rarer still any fresh inquiry into the contribution that a self-consciously American Catholicism might make to the development of this tradition.

The silence imposed by the condemnations of 'Americanism' and Modernism was, of course, broken by Vatican II (1962–65). Within the church in the United States, however, the thrust of the post-Vatican II discussion was already apparent in the groundbreaking work of Fr John Courtney Murray, SJ, whose controversial writings anticipated the Council's recognition of the moral status of religious freedom as the quintessentially human right. Murray's repudiation of Leo XIII's view of church/state relations, in the light of the church's positive experience of the American constitutional separation of the two, helped to redefine not only the basic strategy governing the role of Catholic social teaching in the public arena, but also the diverse ways in which Catholic laity as well as clergy were to become involved in its formulation as well as implementation.

Though Murray can hardly be regarded as the architect of Vatican II's spirit of collegiality within the church, aside from his pioneering insights into these constitutional questions his reflections on the quality of public discourse within both the church and the nation as a whole indirectly facilitated the kind of adult moral dialogue that, a generation after Vatican II, was to become the hallmark of Catholic social teaching in the United States. The dialogical process involved in formulating the recent NCCB pastoral letters, *The Challenge of Peace* (1983) and *Economic Justice for All* (1986), is virtually inconceivable apart from Murray's ideas on what the virtue of civility means for both the church and society as a whole. This process deserves a closer look if we are to understand the revolutionary change that they represent for American Catholicism.

The revolution in communications signified by the pastoral letters is more than a net gain in public relations skills, as if the focus of concern lay with the successful dissemination of church documents. The focus, instead, is quite properly upon the question of authority: that is, the moral authority of the national episcopal conference to contribute as a body to the development of Catholic social teaching. The constraints limiting the exercise of authority in an advanced industrial society are considerable in any case; even more formidable are these in the United States, whose dominant patterns of cultural development are characterized by a spirit of independence and individual liberty so pronounced as to make any form of coherent governance seem pointless. More than a century and a half ago, the essayist Ralph Waldo Emerson canonized 'self-reliance' as the typical American virtue. What this means for communicating Catholic social teaching is that authority must be earned, even within the church and among lay persons who are loyal American Catholics. The teachings of the church will be taken seriously when they are seen to make sense to any reasonable person; otherwise, they will be ignored.

How the authority to teach is to be earned, in American terms, can be understood with respect to one of a number of tendencies associated with this dominant cultural pattern of self-reliance, namely, the American penchant for procedural justice. This tacitly American standard of reasonableness quickly gets specified as the demand for equality of access to public moral argument. Moral authority is conferred upon those teachings that, in their very formulation, take into account the opinions of those most affected by them. Consultative procedures that solicit the participation of all those affected, especially the voices of those normally excluded from public moral argument, are not just prudent and polite, but are essential for conferring legitimacy. The substantive conclusions reached, so Americans tend to think, especially with regard to matters of public policy, are only as valid as the inclusive range of those who were actually party to the discussion. If significant groups, for whatever reason, are denied access to the discussion, its results are received with scepticism, regardless of their substantive merits. Though this point was most recently brought home to me while listening to an Afro-American critique of Catholic social teaching made on behalf of Black Catholics in the United States, it is surely representative of the expectations implicit in the national culture as a whole.

Ironically, the bishops charged with the drafting of the pastoral letters did not initially hit upon the process of consultation through critical reflection on the American ethos. There was an unauthorized leak to the press of the first draft of *The Challenge of Peace* and, not wanting to be trapped in the impossible role of suppressing public response to the first draft, the bishops decided to open up the process of consultation to as wide a public as possible. This new level of openness was also facilitated, again with no little irony, by the bishops' skilful development of the Vatican's own suggestions regarding the role of prudential judgments in Catholic social teaching. Rather than unduly restrict their own teaching authority to matters of principle, as the Congregation and the Doctrine of the Faith may have wished, the bishops identified the legitimacy of dissent from their specific policy recommendations with the category of prudential judgments. As the final draft of *The Challenge of Peace* insisted, in principle prudential judgments define the area in which persons 'in good faith' can legitimately disagree not only with one another but also with their bishops. Consistent with this recognition of the laity's right of legitimate dissent from the bishops' view of Catholic social teaching, the various conclusions regarding the possession and use of nuclear weapons offered by the bishops were qualified in the final draft with reference to the category of prudential judgment. A similar set of assumptions about public moral argument within the church also govern the third chapter of *Economic Justice for All*, on select questions of economic policy.

If the American bishops' recognition of the right of legitimate dissent ensures that the consultative process will in fact be a meaningful one, even more telling for helping the pastoral letters to earn their own moral authority was the way in which the process itself was organized. In both cases, once the decision to accept the opening up of the drafting process was made, the bishops on the drafting committee participated in a series of meetings, some open to the public at large and some not, at which a range of opinions, and not just expert opinion, was presented and subject to critical scrutiny. During the formulation of the drafts of the pastoral letter on the economy, I actively participated in one such meeting, the December 1983 meeting organized by the Notre Dame Center for Ethics and Religious Values in Business, and later observed another, co-sponsored by the Diocese of Oakland, California, and the Jesuit School of Theology at Berkeley. Both meetings featured presenters and panelists, clergy and laity, Catholic and non-Catholic, who represented significant constituencies to be addressed by the pastoral letter: for example, theologians and public policy intellectuals, union officials, business leaders, government bureaucrats and a range of social activists claiming to speak with and for the poor and the marginalized. Significant effort seems to have been made by the meetings' sponsors, in cooperation with staff advisers from the USCC, to ensure that the bishops would be challenged by a diversity of opinion. Opportunity was also provided for the bishops and their advisers from the USCC to cross-examine the testimony of the various speakers. The Notre Dame meeting was especially effective in allowing the bishops ample time to interact with the experts assembled, while the Berkeley meeting allowed for more access for representatives of poor and the marginalized. Given the constraints upon the time available for such meetings, a trade-off between the two may somehow have to be adjudicated for such consultations to be an effective instrument for future pastoral letters.

Besides these consultations, so reminiscent of the American pioneer tradition of a 'town meeting', the resulting series of drafts submitted to the public through the secular and religious press also helped mobilize support for the pastoral letters. Here another dimension of the American standard of reasonableness comes into play: that is, the ability to revise one's own thinking, to accommodate it critically to the legitimate concerns of others holding a different view. Those who participated in the consultative processes, or who wrote personal responses to the various drafts of the letters – and they numbered in the tens of thousands – could see how subsequent drafts were revised in light of their own contributions. Here, too, the pastoral letters earned a hearing for themselves by demonstrating the concrete reasonableness of those responsible for drafting them. One might be tempted to take for granted the quality of participation facilitated by the Catholic press at both the diocesan and national levels; but even more significant, and not just with respect to reaching a non-Catholic audience, was the news coverage and analyses offered in the secular news media. It is probable that more American Catholics were informed by the secular media about both letters' contents, that were actually reached either through the Catholic press or through various diocesan and parish level educational programs designed to disseminate their teachings.

The scale and scope of secular news coverage was unprecedented in the history of the church in the United States. What provoked this level of interest, in my opinion, was not simply the intrinsic merits of the topics discussed in the pastoral letters, but more importantly the dynamism of the process of drafting the letters. A consultative process aspiring to genuine openness in a church rightly or wrongly perceived by the public as often less than open, a claim to authority based upon the peculiarly forceless force of better public arguments, and the drama of ongoing dissent within a church actively seeking moral consensus on a new basis – all of these helped to define the secular press's interest, and especially to sustain it from one draft to another. Of course, the convergence and divergence of the pastoral letters' policy recommendations from those offered by the major political parties in the United States was also a crucial factor, especially at a time when the nation seemed to be witnessing a significant long-term realignment of these parties in national politics. More than one commentator hinted that now was 'the Catholic moment', in so far as how Catholics made up their minds about certain key issues, ranging from national defence to social welfare entitlements, would be decisive for shaping a new majority in American politics. The various drafts of the letters thus received an inordinate amount of attention to the details of their specific policy recommendations among those pundits determined to predict which way the Catholic vote would go.

I conclude this brief report by outlining some of the problems involved in the pastoral process. No process is trouble-free, of course; the important question is which set of problems the church is willing to live with in advancing the cause of Catholic social teaching. For the very strengths of the drafting process give evidence of significant weaknesses. First, consider the question of authority. If a new kind of moral authority was earned by opening up the drafting process to public participation, a question arises concerning the relationship between the new and more traditional understandings of episcopal authority. On one level, this is the familiar question of the teaching authority (*mandatum docendi*) of the episcopal conference as such. Is there such an authority, and if so, how can it be implemented without undermining the authority of the individual bishop in his own diocese? The seeming paradox involved in the notion of earned authority is at another level. Is this authority more apparent than real? Does it not reduce the basis of the church's teaching authority to a purely procedural notion of competence in facilitating public dialogue? Clearly, the openness of the drafting process, and the unusual spectacle of

Catholic bishops revising their opinions in the light of lay and secular criticism, involves the risk of succumbing to an empty proceduralism. Is the risk worth it?

A related problem is the unforeseeable risk of distortion involved in allowing the secular news media, willy-nilly, to become the primary vehicle for communicating Catholic social teaching to ordinary Catholics. The press coverage of the various drafts of the pastoral letters was, alas, uneven. It tended to ebb and flow according to the rhythm of electoral politics in the United States. One troubling outcome was that such coverage tended to over-emphasize the importance of the first draft of each letter, and to discount the significance of the final draft. This tendency, if unchecked, will lessen the moral legitimacy to be gained by opening up the drafting process, precisely because the first draft, of its very nature, is less likely to be fully representative of the range of opinion within the church as a whole. The first drafts, in both cases, were the most controversial, and most subject to challenge because of ideological bias; the final drafts, which reflected the bishops' desire to achieve the widest possible consensus, less so. Here, too, the question is one of authority: precisely which draft of the pastoral letters comes to be regarded by the public as authoritative? Common sense and ecclesiology demand that the final draft formally accepted by the episcopal conference as a whole be regarded as authoritative. But this, arguably, is not the result of a process whose outcomes are communicated most effectively by the secular news media.

Finally, a deeper level to the question of ideological bias must be confronted. Is the ideal of open discussion itself but an ideological façade masking the bureaucratic power of special interests that allegedly dominate the USCC? Neo-conservative critics of the pastoral letters, both the process and its substantive outcomes, repeatedly raised this question. What moved them to do so, ultimately, was a dubious hypothesis launched by sociologist, Peter Berger, concerning the emergence of a 'new class' bent on dominating key institutions in advanced industrial societies. This 'new class' is identified with the production and dissemination of socially useful 'knowledge' that defines, to the 'new class's' own benefit, the ways in which economic and social policy questions and the legitimate range of answers to them are framed for public discussion. The political tendency of the 'new class', according to the neo-conservative view, is hardly innocent. It is generally liberal; indeed, it defines the extremity of liberalism on the spectrum of public opinion in the United States. The 'new class' thus stands accused of being hostile or indifferent to the exercise of traditional forms of authority, which derive from sources other than its own distinct form of 'knowledge'.

There is no question that an advanced industrial society, especially a democracy that embraces cultural diversity as a fundamental value, places a premium on the work of those who mediate symbolically among a plurality of such perspectives. At issue here, however, is whether these symbolic analysts form a distinct social class complete with a defining class interest; and if in general they do, whether the church itself has become captive to them. The neo-conservative critique of the pastoral letter process thus focussed on the role of the staff support provided by the USCC, claiming – somewhat implausibly, in my view – that these bureaucrats manipulated the process's outcome by controlling the bishops' access to expert opinion, especially on the public policy questions addressed in the letters. Only those economists and other social scientists, so the accusation read, whose 'knowledge' of societal reality corresponded to views already held by USCC staff, were given a serious opportunity to influence the bishops drafting the pastoral letters. The fact that the 'town meetings' also featured representatives speaking with and for the poor and the marginalized, in the neo-conservative view, merely confirmed the accusation. For here the bishops were doubly manipulated, as only politically correct spokespersons were granted access to the bishops. Indeed, so deep was the neo-conservative animus against the pastoral letters process that in both cases self-appointed 'lay commissions' conducted their own independent hearings and issued their own counter-pastoral letters.

While the neo-conservative complaint simply will not survive detailed scrutiny of what actually went on in the 'town meetings', it does not suggest that there are limits to what reasonably can be expected from opening the drafting process to unrestricted participation. The tension between insiders and those outside the process may be slackened, but it cannot be eliminated. Furthermore, self-consciously ideological conflict will inevitably tend to be intensified within the church, whenever such a process is undertaken. Persons and groups will be mobilized to gain a hearing for their particular point of view, and the bishops' staff advisers will necessarily have the responsibility of exercising some degree of control even over a dialogical process that aspires to genuine openness. Those who participate in such a process must steel themselves for exposure to ideological combat. The only way to avoid completely the kind of ideological crossfire in which American neo-conservatives hoped to trap the pastoral letters is for the bishops to refrain from making any specific policy recommendations whatsoever. But surely this is to surrender the tradition of Catholic social teaching at precisely its most effective point of challenge.

Despite these problems, the basic thrust of the American Catholic bishops' pastoral letter process needs to be preserved and tested further. The bishops stumbled upon an important discovery, essential for communicating Catholic social teaching in the United States, and possibly relevant for the church's mission in other countries as well. That discovery is the emerging realization that ordinary Catholics are likely to identify with the tradition only if they are allowed access to the processes in which it is continually being reassessed and reformulated. They are not likely to accept passively instruction in a moral perspective that they had no hand in shaping. In order for the church to facilitate this new style of adult learning, it will itself have to learn how to become a community of moral discourse. Rather than abandon Catholic social teaching's traditional readiness to speak boldly on specific questions of public policy, the church should reconsider the nature of Christian moral education and routinely facilitate adult moral dialogue, involving laity as well as clergy, within its own educational practices. The recent experience of the church in the United States certainly provides no easy answers as to the shape of this educational reform, but the open consultative process marking the NCCB's recent pastoral letters is promising enough to be considered seriously for implementation elsewhere in the church.

Contributors

MICHAEL SCHÄFERS was born in Westphalia in 1962. He studied theology, social sciences and educational theory, and since 1989 has been working for his doctorate on 'The Prophetic Power of Catholic Social Teaching' in the University/Gesamthochschule of Paderborn. His research relates to the origin and development of church social teaching; work, property and the criticism of the business world in Catholic social teaching; and new concepts of social politics and their significance for the worldwide problem of poverty.

JOSÉ MARÍA DÍEZ-ALEGRÍA was born in Gijón in Spain in 1911. He holds a bachelor's degree in theology and doctorate in philosophy from the Gregorian and in law from Madrid University. He taught ethics at the Jesuit faculty of philosophy in Madrid from 1947 to 1961, and social sciences at the Gregorian from 1961 to 1973. His best-known work is *Yo creo en la esperanza* (1972), which was translated into English, French, Italian and German. His latest books are *La cara oculta del cristianismo* (1983), *¿Se puede ser cristiano en esta iglesia?* (1987), and *Cristianismo y propiedad privada* (1988).

NORBERT METTE was born in 1946 in Barkhausen/Porta. He studied theology and social sciences and gained his doctorate in theology. Since 1984 he has been Professor of Practical Theology at the University/Gesamthochschule of Paderborn. He is married with three children. A member of the Board of Directors of *Concilium*, he has written numerous books and articles on pastoral theology and religious education. These include *Voraussetzungen christlicher Elementarerziehung* (1983) and *Kirche auf dem Weg ins Jahr 2000* (with M. Blasberg-Kuhnke, 1986). With C. Bäumler he has edited *Gemeindepraxis in Grundbegriffen* (1987), and with P. Eicher, *Auf der Seite der Unterdrückten? Theologie der Befreiung im Kontext Europas* (1989).

JOHN A. GALLAGHER is Director of Corporate Ethics for the Holy Cross Health System, South Bend, Indiana. He received his doctorate from the

University of Chicago Divinity School and has taught at Mercy College of Detroit and Loyola University of Chicago. He is the author of *Time Past, Time Future*, a study of the neo-Thomist manuals of moral theology.

MICHAEL J. SCHUCK was born in Fargo, North Dakota in 1953. After studying history and political science at St Louis University and the University of Chicago, he gained a PhD in ethics from the University of Chicago in 1988. He is currently Assistant Professor of Theological Ethics in the Department of Theology at Loyola University, Chicago. His book, *That They Be One: The Social Teaching of the Papal Encyclicals 1740–1989*, was published by Georgetown University Press in 1991.

GREGORY BAUM was born in Berlin in 1923; since 1940 he has lived in Canada. He studied at McMaster University in Hamilton, Ontario; Ohio State University; the University of Fribourg, Switzerland; and the New School for Social Research in New York. He is Master of Arts and Doctor of Theology and is now Professor of Theology and Social Ethics at McGill University, Montreal. He is editor of *The Ecumenist*. His publications include *Religion and Alienation* (1975); *The Social Imperative* (1978); *Catholics and Canadian Socialism* (1980); *The Priority of Labor* (1982); *Ethics and Economics* (1984); and *Theology and Society* (1987).

STEPHAN H. P. PFÜRTNER was born in Danzig in 1922. From 1939–1943 he studied medicine and from 1945–54 philosophy and theology at Walberberg, Fribourg (Switzerland) and Rome, where he gained his doctorate in 1954. After lecturing in anthropology and ethics, in 1961 he became Rector of Walberberg Hochschule, moving to the University of Fribourg in 1966 as Professor of Moral Theology. Between 1962 and 1969 he built up and directed the Walberberg Jugendakademie. From 1975 to 1988 he was Professor of Social Ethics at the Philipps-Universität, Marburg. He is married, with two children. His publications include *Triebleben und sittliche Vollendung* (1958); *Luther and Thomas on Salvation* (1965); and *Kirche und Sexualität* (1975). He edited the first eight volumes of the *Internationale Ökumenische Bibliographie* (1967–1969); with N. Luhmann he edited *Theorie, Technik und Moral* (1978), and with W. Heierle, *Einführung in die Katholische Soziallehre*; with the latter he also edited and wrote the two-volume *Ethik in der europäischen Geschichte* (1988).

ALBERTO MELLONI was born in Reggio Emilia in 1959. He studied at the University of Bologna; Cornell University, Ithaca NY; and the Catholic

University of Fribourg, Switzerland. He is a church historian and works at the Institute for Religious Sciences at Bologna. He has taken an active part in its research projects (on John XXIII, Christianity, African Christianity and Vatican II), contributing numerous articles to academic journals and other works. He edited the critical edition of Pope John's *Journal of a Soul* (Bologna 1987) and is interested in ecclesiology (*Innocenzo IV*, Genoa 1990). He is editor of the review *Cristianesimo nella storia*.

MARIA LIBISZOWSKA-ZOLTKOWSKA is a sociologist and works at the Institute of Philosophy and Sociology of the Polish Academy of Science in Warsaw. Her doctorate is in the sociology of religion. The main areas of her work include the general theoretical and methodological problems of the sociology of religion and empirical research (most recently into the treatment of the intelligentsia by religion). She has published some articles in Polish periodicals.

MARIA RILEY OP is a Dominican sister from Adrian, Michigan. She is currently a research associate on women's issues at the Center of Concern in Washington, DC. In addition to regular speaking and workshop engagements, she is the author of *Transforming Feminism*; other works include *Wisdom Seeks Her Way: Liberating the Power of Women's Spirituality*, *In God's Image*, and *Women Faithful for the Future*. Her *I am Because We Are* focusses on the three goals of the United Nations International Women's Decade: Equality, Development and Peace. With Nancy Sylvester IHM of Network she has recently written *Trouble and Beauty: Women Encounter Catholic Social Teaching*; this process book, written to celebrate 100 years of Catholic social teaching, is a collaborative work of the Center of Concern, Leadership Conference of Women Religious, and Network.

RICARDO ANTONCICH is a Jesuit, born in Peru in 1931. After studying philosophy in Spain and theology in Frankfurt, he returned to Peru to work in the Bishops' Commission for Social Work and the theology department of the Catholic University of Lima. Since 1976 he has worked in several Latin American countries as adviser to CLAR and CELAM. He has written two books on spirituality and three on social teaching: *Christians in the Face of Injustice* (1987), *La doctrina social de la Iglesia* (1987), and *Trabajo y Libertad* (1988).

DENNIS P. MCCANN is Professor of Religious Studies and Co-Director of the Center for the Study of Values at De Paul University, Chicago. He received his STL in theology from the Gregorian University in Rome in 1971 and a PhD in theology from the University of Chicago Divinity School in 1976. His publications include *Christian Realism and Liberation Theology*, Maryknoll 1981; *New Experiment in Democracy: The Challenge for American Catholicism*, Kansas City 1987; and, with Charles R. Strain, *Polity and Praxis: A Program for American Practical Theology*, New York 1985, reprinted 1990.

Members of the Advisory Committee for Sociology of Religion

Directors

Gregory Baum	Montreal	Canada
John Coleman SJ	Berkeley, CA	USA

Members

Sabino Acquaviva	Padua	Italy
Silvano Burgalassi	Pisa	Italy
Joan Chittister OSB	Erie, PA	USA
Gérard Defois	Paris	France
Karel Dobbelaere	Louvain	Belgium
Jacques Grand'Maison	Montreal	Canada
Andrew Greeley	Chicago, IL	USA
Barbara Hargrove	Denver, CO	USA
Franz-Xavier Kaufmann	Bielefeld	Germany
Leonardus Laeyendecker	Leiden	The Netherlands
David Martin	London	Great Britain
Peter McAffery	Old Aberdeen	Great Britain
Meredith McGuire	San Antonio, TX	USA
Ferdinand Menne	Münster	Germany
John Orme Mills OP	Oxford	Great Britain
Hans Mol	Hamilton, Ont.	Canada
Marie Neal SND	Boston, MA	USA
Jean Remy	Louvain-la-Neuve	Belgium
Rudolf Siebert	Kalamazoo, MI	USA
Jean-Guy Vaillancourt	Montreal	Canada
Conor Ward	Dublin	Ireland

Concilium Editorial Board

Bestsellers from SCM Press and TPI

Strenuous Commands
The Ethic of Jesus
A E Harvey
'I commend this book to every minister and to all who are concerned about the teaching of Jesus. By asking within what framework of thought this teaching would have been given and what response it would have awakened in the hearers, Harvey opens up the ethic of Jesus in a way which is genuinely fresh and new.'
(Expository Times)

Creation out of Nothing
Don Cupitt
'In a Decade of Evangelism religious leaders should read this book. Cupitt maps out a brief history of modern thought and explains how language creates God in our own image . . . If you want an introduction to modern philosophy and literary theory here's a good start.'
(Reform)

Many Tables
The Eucharist in the New Testament and Liturgy Today
Dennis E Smith and Hal E Taussig
'It is highly refreshing to have a study of eucharistic origins written from a standpoint that is not firmly conservative . . . Members of the Liturgical Commission and of diocesan liturgical committees should certainly place this book firmly on their reading lists.'
(Church Times)

Jesus Christ in Modern Thought
John Macquarrie
' . . a useful survey of the field, and a christology for post- Enlightenment men and women . . . It is a resource and reference book to buy and to refer to often.'
(Expository Times)

The Birth of Modern Critical Theology
Characters and problems of biblical criticism in the seventeenth century
Klaus Scholder
'Scholder's work has been central to the development of theories about the devolopment of historical criticism and its influence upon theology . . . It is important and illuminating, and will join other central works in this area.'
(Theological Book Review)

Marx and the Failure of Liberation Theology
Alistair Kee
'This serious book deserves a welcome, with admiration for its great skill in combining careful and extensive scholarship (in Marxist and Latin American fields alike) with a style which is lucid, energetic and readable, stimulating international dialogue at the required level.'
(Church Times)

Theology Today
Jürgen Moltmann
'There are many touches of a master's hand. Dr Moltmann has written a long series of books making him more or less the equal of the great men he discusses.'
(Church Times)

Creating a Just Future
The Politics of Peace and the Ethics of Creation in a Threatened World
Jürgen Moltmann
'It is full of valuable political as well as theological insights: it is also very readable and clear.'
(The Way)

The Poet, The Warrior, The Prophet
Rubem A. Alves
'It seems churlish to attempt formal criticism of a work which must have come as a gift to the audience of the Edward Cadbury Lectures 1990. Gifts are either shunted off to the Oxfam shop or enjoyed. This book was a joy.'
(Theology)

The Johannine Question
Martin Hengel
'Hengel's theory is fascinatingly unravelled and supported by exact scholarship . . . this is a book to ponder.'
(Biblical Studies)

The Theology of a Protestant Catholic
Adrian Hastings
'These occasional writings . . . cover a good deal of ground, combining a stark realism with an underlying hope; academic rigour with commitment to the community of faith; provisionality – with conviction; and an analytic coolness with controlled passion and occasional lyricism.'
(Church Times)

African Catholicism
Essays in Discovery
Adrian Hastings
' . . . the book has a coherence, an impact and an urgency very rare in such collections . . . this book is a work of exceptional authority and importance, essential reading for all who love Africa and fear for its future.'
(The Way)

A Dictionary of Biblical Interpretation
ed R J Coggins and J L Houlden
'If you dip into this book, you will find yourself "hooked", fascinated in its original literal sense: for wherever may be your starting point, the admirably full cross referencing system leads you on a tour which takes you to new insights and unfamiliar territory, and on the way you will find in impossible to pass by some very alluring topic!'
(The Expository Times)

On Presence
Ralph Harper
A rich, captivating and distinctive book that demonstrates a lifetime of learning. The author explores the idea of 'presence' or 'being' through a wide range of writers, combining the concrete phenomenological sensitivities of Marcel or Buber with the kind of meditational readings of literary texts found in the late Heidegger.

The Faith Factor in Healing
Thomas A Droege
A book about health and spirituality, regarding both as complimentary aspects of whole person health care. A stimulating account that broadens the understanding and awe of the healing process.

Theology at the End of Modernity
ed. Sheila Greeve Davaney
Analyses the current state of theology as modernity draws to a close and sets an agenda for theological reflection to pursue into the next century.

Jews and Christians
Getting Our Stories Straight
Michael Goldberg
A literary and theological commentary on the exodus and the resurrection. 'A welcome contribution both to theology and interfaith understanding. Deserves to be read by laity and scholars alike.' (Jon D Levenson, Harvard Divinity School)

Questions of Faith

ed. Dolly K Patterson

An extraordinary book by extraordinary people in response to age-old questions concerning God, prayer, good, evil, organized religion, Jesus, the Bible, truth and justice, meaning and faith, and death.
Winner of the 1991 Public Relations Council's Wilbur Award in the 'Best Book' category.

Faith and Piety in Early Judaism

Texts and Documents

George W E Nickelsburg and Michael E Stone

A revealing collection of texts and documents from Second-Temple Jerusalem, showing the Judaism of that period to be remarkable not only as a fertile seed-bed for later developments, but as a vital religion of profound creativity and rich diversity in its own right.

The Pleasure of Her Text

Feminist Readings of Biblical and Historical Texts

ed Alice Bach

A collection of articles by leading female scholars, which shows that there is no such thing as a single message of feminist hermeneutics, but rather a gloriously rich diversity of style and comment which points the way toward salvaging many submerged female voices.

Biography as Theology

How Life Stories Can Remake Today's Theology

James Wm McClendon Jr

A classic of the narrative theology movement, this book considers the lives of Dag Hammarskjöld and Martin Luther King Jr in an effort to show how biography **is** theology.

Available in America from: Trinity Press International
3725 Chestnut Street
Philadelphia
PA 19104
USA
